# ENGAGING MINDS
## IN THE Classroom

*Engaging Minds in English Language Arts Classrooms: The Surprising Power of Joy*
by Mary Jo Fresch,
edited by Michael F. Opitz and Michael P. Ford

*Engaging Minds in Science and Math Classrooms: The Surprising Power of Joy*
by Eric Brunsell and Michelle A. Fleming,
edited by Michael F. Opitz and Michael P. Ford

*Engaging Minds in Social Studies Classrooms: The Surprising Power of Joy*
by James A. Erekson,
edited by Michael F. Opitz and Michael P. Ford

# ENGAGING MINDS
## IN THE Classroom

## THE SURPRISING POWER OF **JOY**

**MICHAEL F. OPITZ**

**MICHAEL P. FORD**

Alexandria, Virginia USA

1703 N. Beauregard St. • Alexandria, VA 22311-1714 USA
Phone: 800-933-2723 or 703-578-9600 • Fax: 703-575-5400
Website: www.ascd.org • E-mail: member@ascd.org
Author guidelines: www.ascd.org/write

Gene R. Carter, *Executive Director;* Richard Papale, *Acting Chief Program Development Officer;* Stefani Roth, *Interim Publisher;* Laura Lawson and Stefani Roth, *Acquisitions Editors;* Julie Houtz, *Director, Book Editing & Production;* Darcie Russell, *Senior Associate Editor;* Georgia Park, *Senior Graphic Designer;* Mike Kalyan, *Production Manager;* Barton Matheson Willse & Worthington, *Typesetter;* Andrea Wilson, *Production Specialist*

PAPERBACK ISBN: 978-1-4166-1633-7    ASCD product #113020                    n1/14
Also available as an e-book (see Books in Print for the ISBNs).

Quantity discounts: 10–49 copies, 10%; 50+ copies, 15%; for 1,000 or more copies, call 800-933-2723, ext. 5634, or 703-575-5634. For desk copies: www.ascd.org/deskcopy

**Library of Congress Cataloging-in-Publication Data**
Opitz, Michael F.
  Engaging minds in the classroom : the surprising power of joy / Michael F. Opitz and Michael P. Ford.
     pages cm.
  Includes bibliographical references and index.
  ISBN 978-1-4166-1633-7 (pbk. : alk. paper)  1. Motivation in education.
2. Affective education.  3. Emotions and cognition.  4. Joy.  I. Ford, Michael P.  II. Title.
  LB1065.O54 2014
  370.15'4—dc23
                                                                    2013031416

23 22 21 20 19 18 17 16 15 14          1 2 3 4 5 6 7 8 9 10 11 12

# ENGAGING MINDS
## in the Classroom

## THE SURPRISING POWER OF **JOY**

Acknowledgments. . . . . . . . . . . . . . . . . . . . . . . . . . . . . . . . . . vii

Introduction . . . . . . . . . . . . . . . . . . . . . . . . . . . . . . . . . . . . . . .1

1. Understanding Joyful Learning . . . . . . . . . . . . . . . . . . . . . . .7

2. Assessing and Evaluating Joyful Learning . . . . . . . . . . . . . . .24

3. Implementing Joyful Learning. . . . . . . . . . . . . . . . . . . . . . . .47

4. Using Joyful Learning to Support
   Education Initiatives . . . . . . . . . . . . . . . . . . . . . . . . . . . . . .63

   References . . . . . . . . . . . . . . . . . . . . . . . . . . . . . . . . . . . . . .70

   Index. . . . . . . . . . . . . . . . . . . . . . . . . . . . . . . . . . . . . . . . . .74

   About the Authors. . . . . . . . . . . . . . . . . . . . . . . . . . . . . . . .77

# Acknowledgments

We wish to thank the many individuals who were involved in the making of this book and the companion titles.

The authors of the companion books bring joyful learning to specific content areas: Eric Brunsell, associate professor at the University of Wisconsin, and Michelle Fleming, assistant professor at Wright State University, mathematics and science; James Erekson, associate professor at the University of Northern Colorado, social studies; and Mary Jo Fresch, professor at Ohio State University, language arts. We appreciate their contributions and their passion for the importance of making learning an enjoyable experience.

Lindsey Moses, assistant professor at Arizona State University, wrote many of the teaching tips, focusing on reaching the diversity of learners in today's classroom, for this book and its companion titles. We appreciate her thoughtful read of each manuscript, which resulted in the pertinent details she offers to readers who are likely teaching English language learners in their classrooms.

Conversations about rediscovering joyous effort in classrooms began in work with colleague Leslie McClain, professor at the University of Wisconsin–Stevens Point, who generously shared her resources and thoughts as we shaped our initial ideas.

Many individuals at ASCD saw the need for this project and helped us bring it to fruition. Laura Lawson and Stefani Roth, acquisitions editors, brought clarity to the book that you now hold. We also acknowledge the editing, production, design, and typesetting work that was led by Allison Scott, Darcie Russell, Andrea Wilson, Georgia Park, and Louise Davis.

We also wish to acknowledge our wives, Sheryl and Pat, for the joy they bring us in our lives.

# Introduction

At the end of the professional conference session, we follow our usual routine of putting away materials, shutting down the computer, and talking with participants who approach us for more information. More than one person thanks us for making it so enjoyable; one woman says,

> You look like you enjoy the content, enjoy presenting with one another, and enjoy all the people in the room. Your enjoyment is contagious! Thank you for not only sharing meaningful content, but also showing and reminding us that when we as teachers enjoy what we are teaching and those we are teaching, our students are likely to sense this enjoyment and therefore enjoy learning.

We leave the room feeling euphoric, as evidenced by our laughter and light footsteps.

Our typical routine includes reflecting on the session; in this case, we talk about how the comments about joy took us by surprise. What did we do that expressed and transmitted our joy to our audience? We realize that we have just uncovered another important question to explore: what is *joyful learning*?

We can hear the cynics already: "Joyful learning? In this day and age of accountability and standardization, you are asking educators to seriously consider focusing on bringing joy to classroom teaching and learning? You must be kidding!"

Actually, we're not. We believe there is a place for joyful learning—and joyful teaching—in today's classroom.

Borrowing a page from curriculum theorist Madeline Grumet (1999) when she made her case for the rediscovery of romance in research, we, too, could tweak the lyrics of Lyle and Britten's "What's Love Got to Do with It" (1984) to express why educators should focus on bringing joy to teaching and learning. What's joy got to do with it? Is there good reason to be mindful of joyful learning, especially in a climate that equates education attainment with high test scores? *Isn't joy just a secondhand outcome?* In short, why bother with joyful teaching and learning? *Who needs joy when joy isn't tested?*

Joy seems to be elusive in most classrooms. In an era of increased accountability and standardization, joy seems to have all but disappeared. Portrayals of school and school personnel in popular culture are often negative and laughable, as in the automaticity of the economics teacher in *Ferris Bueller's Day Off* (1986), who repeats "Anyone? Anyone?" after many of his questions. Even in books for younger children, the prospect of school seems joyless, not joyful. The subtitle of Neal Layton's picture book *The Sunday Blues: A Book for Schoolchildren, Schoolteachers, and Anybody Else Who Dreads Monday Mornings* (2002) says it all. But should school be something everyone dreads? Isn't there a way to rediscover the joy of teaching and learning in today's schools? Could we eliminate the dread and focus on the joy that Layton's character experiences after arriving at school and being surrounded by his friends?

## Considering Noncognitive Skills of Learning

The affective dimensions of teaching and learning—what some educators are now calling "noncognitive, academic skills" (Tough, 2012, p. 161)—are often overlooked. These affective dimensions include feelings, emotions, self-esteem. Clearly short-changed in a period focused on the cognitive aspects of schooling, we need to acknowledge that noncognitive skills have thoughtful, reflective components that include conscientiousness, grit, self-control, curiosity, persistence, optimism, and interpersonal skills. In our research on joyful learning, motivation (i.e., what motivates students to learn in classrooms), and engagement, we have discovered that many researchers and theorists have also considered the need to rethink learning and teaching experiences that are not intentionally focused on affective outcomes. As Tough (2012) made clear, if we truly want to advance the learning of all students, we need to seriously consider how noncognitive skills influence learning.

As part of our postsession discussion, we also reflect on and discuss our own teaching and learning experiences. In addition to the obvious joy in our collaborative work, highlighted by that teacher in our audience, we each can point to examples of joy in our own histories of teaching and learning. Mike Ford recalls Jim Cook, an amazing freshman physical science teacher, who would lean on his desk, lock eyes with him, and say, "Ford, I know you know the answer. It starts with a *b*." Mr. Cook helped his students find the joy in that content and gave us the feeling that he found *his* greatest joy in that classroom. Recently, upon returning from a family trip to Disney World, my 1st grade student Ariel wrote in her journal, "I hope I don't have to do that again"—because she missed school so much. When school is more joyous than Disney World, something good must be happening.

Mike Opitz had a class with Toby Edson, an outstanding history of education professor. Up to that point, he had never taken any pleasure in history of any kind (as evidenced when playing Trivial Pursuit or watching *Jeopardy*). Edson made history live through his passion for the topic; his interactive lectures were peppered with examples about how history is a story constructed by the history teller (i.e., historiographer). Opitz was so taken with Edson's teaching that he read nearly every book that Edson mentioned and seriously considered doing a historiography for his advanced degree. Perhaps the most heart-felt story is from Opitz's former kindergarten student, who wrote this note as she was preparing to become a teacher:

> I don't know if you remember me since it was so long ago (1986/87), but I definitely remember you. I still remember most of the songs we sang in class, the fun we had, and I even remember the kindergarten graduation. The fun I had in kindergarten is one reason why I am passionate about the teaching profession for myself.

## Joyful Teaching and Learning

We believe in the idea of *principled practice*—practice informed by both our professional experiences and consensus of expert opinion and research from the field (Vogt & Shearer, 2010). As we look for insights and ideas to move our thinking and practices forward, we consider not only the consensus of expert opinion and research from the field, but also acknowledge our own experiences and professional wisdom. Research and experience have led us to the information that forms the content of this book and its companion titles on math and science, language arts, and social studies. We want to help you uncover ways to take this information and apply it to your own unique teaching experience.

Fortunately, this information will fit into your existing classroom routines; much of it is more about your mindset about learners, content, and teaching than it is about adding new content to your already overstuffed curricula. Our aim is to make this book and its companions practical, easy to use, and accessible.

Chapter 1 presents a framework for joyful learning to use in teaching and learning experiences every day. In addition to defining *joyful learning*, we discuss motivation theories and current thinking about engagement, and the importance of these noncognitive factors in learning.

In Chapter 2, we explore the importance of assessment and evaluation. We consider in particular five elements that need to be assessed and evaluated in order to get the most from joyful learning: learners, teachers, texts and materials, assessments, and schoolwide configurations. Finally, we offer two assessment surveys that individual teachers and the entire school staff can use to assess and evaluate the elements. We also offer some suggestions about how to compile and use the findings.

Implementing joyful learning is the focus of Chapter 3. We identify and discuss the five essential configurations that can help promote joyful learning: school community, physical environment, whole-group instruction, small-group instruction, and individual instruction. We also suggest specific learning activities that fit within the joyful learning–structured classroom. Collectively, all structures and activities contribute to our joyful learning framework.

Contemporary demands have been the mainstay of our combined 60 years of teaching. For example, Response to Intervention (RTI) and the common core state standards (CCSS) are two current demands on educators. We predict that there will always be contemporary demands that call for teacher attention. Our experience has been that when we attend to the demand as a process of incorporating the trend into what we are currently doing, rather than letting the demand overtake us (or our students), we are able to take the best components from the demand and use it to reach more learners. We provide some ideas for how to do so in Chapter 4.

## Reaching All Students

Most teachers today work in increasingly diverse classrooms that include students of varying abilities and learning challenges and those who are English language learners (ELLs). What we use to teach and the contexts in which we teach need to be both mirrors and windows for *all* learners. They deserve nothing less. All children need to see themselves in the materials we use and the classroom environments in which they live to bring about joyful learning. This means paying close attention as we select books (and other texts for the classroom library) or media for our own use or to present to students. It means being more intentional in filling our physical spaces as celebrations that represent the lives of all represented in any given classroom and school.

The ability to see into the lives of others in those same materials and environments also helps build a sense of community that contributes to joyful learning. In reporting on the firsthand accounts of ELLs, Jimenez (1999) noted that joyful learning surfaces when students feel successful and when their success is genuinely recognized by others. His findings underscore the importance of providing scaffolds for success, helping create a value for the activity, and providing a safe atmosphere in which to operate.

For this reason, throughout this book we offer teaching tips that highlight how the content best connects with diverse learners. Let's be clear: We believe that good instruction transcends demographic groups. We also believe that ELLs and students of different academic abilities and challenges should be considered central to classroom populations rather than afterthoughts.

Perhaps David Pearson's comments capture our sentiment the best: "Kids are who they are. They know what they know. They bring what they bring. And we need to stop seeing this as an instructional inconvenience" (1996). We remain steadfast in our belief that focusing on the whole child, whoever that child might be, is a sure way to help all students rediscover the joy of learning.

Gail Small noted, "If you can bring your joys and passions into your classroom, your students will be encouraged to find and express theirs" (2003, p. 139). We agree. We also wholeheartedly believe that attending to joyful learning in every sense of how we define it within this book and companion titles is the best way to bring out the best in students and in ourselves. As a result of reading this book and the others that follow, you'll discover exactly what joy has to do with it!

# Understanding Joyful Learning

In the teachers' lounge, Mary and Mike are discussing their day when 5th grade teacher Kathy enters the room. "I planned a great social studies lesson. I pulled things off the web that I thought would spark discussion, but my kids sat there like rocks. What else can I do?"

"I seem to be the only one working in my classroom." says Mary, who teaches 6th grade. "I am trying to show how writing can be enjoyable, but I'm not succeeding. They only seem concerned about how many pages they need to write and the due date. The only enjoyment they seem to find in writing is getting finished."

"I've noticed the same thing," says Mike, a 4th grade teacher. "Many of my students hate math, and I am not really sure why or if I can convince them otherwise."

"What's so frustrating to me is that most of the students have the skills—they just don't seem to care much about applying them," Mary adds. "Maybe I'm sending mixed messages. Some days I am all about selling the love of learning. Other days I am preoccupied with getting them ready for the next round of tests. Maybe we need to take some time to explore ways to create some passion, to make learning more joyful."

"I think you might be onto something," Mike agrees.

Kathy nods, "I'm so busy trying to cover content that I haven't even thought about the joy."

"How about if we search out different ideas, try them out, and come back together to share?" Mary suggests. All agree that a collaborative plan aimed at helping students rediscover the joy of learning is worth pursuing and schedule their first meeting.

Teachers often grapple more with the challenges of the noncognitive, affective dimensions of learning and teaching than with the cognitive aspects. In fact, when we ask teachers what their number one concern is surrounding teaching and learning, they more often than not identify motivation and engagement. For many teachers, their greatest concern is how to engage their students. They know that if students want to learn, success is likely to follow.

When we delve deeper into why motivation and engagement are such a concern, three reasons surface. First, teachers believe (and rightly so) that education enables individuals to live more fulfilled lives. They talk at length about the knowledge, skills, and dispositions that will be required of students for them to lead fulfilling lives. Teachers know that supporting students to become *lifelong learners* (learning how to learn and wanting to continue to learn) will be crucial in a world in which they will need to be able to keep up with and embrace rapid changes. We only need to look at recent changes in technology for one example. In the words of one teacher, "We don't know what our students will be encountering in the future. So we need to help students see the value of learning and how it will contribute to their lives."

A second reason teachers focus on motivation is that they have experienced the pleasure associated with learning and they want to pass these feelings of pleasurable learning—a form of intrinsic motivation—along to their students. Like our own stories in the Introduction, and like the stories of writers who contributed to Sell's *A Cup of Comfort for Teachers* (2007), most teachers have stories about teachers who were powerful influences on their lives. Many became teachers to pass on those same feelings to their students. They wonder, how did their teachers motivate them? And can they as teachers emulate these practices so that their students can experience joyful learning?

Third, given the current focus on accountability—and particularly the linking of student performance to teacher salaries and their continued employment—teachers' job security may be affected by students' motivation to learn. The irony is that because teachers feel pressured to get students to perform on state tests, they are sometimes their own worst enemy when it comes to motivating students. For example, given the pressure to perform in a short amount of time, teachers may present material in a way that students perceive as boring and without meaning or purpose, and students are therefore not motivated to learn. As Cushman (2010) reported,

> The most boring material students had in class, they told me, was often directly linked to high-stakes standardized tests they would be taking. Kids could tell that their teachers worried about tilting the balance toward fun activities at the expense of "rigorous" material that might be on the test. (p. 111)

Often education policy leads us away from addressing affective concerns such as developing a desire to learn content and an appreciation for what is being learned (Brophy, 2008). In the end, ignoring the affective development of our students leaves us further from accomplishing academic goals. Consider what has happened since the No Child Left Behind Act (2001) and its accompanying mandates. In our desk-bound "race to the top," recess is often cut and physical education, art, and music programs are scaled back, if they exist at all. In their place are more content classes perceived to be more rigorous and important to helping students pass high-stakes tests. As Willis (2007) noted, "In their zeal to raise test scores, too many policymakers wrongly assume that students who are laughing, interacting in groups, or being creative with art, music, or dance are not doing *real* academic work" (p. 1).

Yet there is compelling evidence that recess, PE, art, and music activities can help improve students' academic achievement. For example, students who get fitness-oriented classes in lieu of extra "academic" classes outperform those who take the extra classes to the exclusion of participating in fitness classes (Castelli, Hillman, Buck, & Erwin, 2007; Centers for Disease Control and Prevention, 2010; Medina, 2008; Ratey, 2008).

Other important evidence is found in the field of neuroscience. Neuro-imaging and neurochemical researchers' findings suggest that enjoyable classroom experiences that capitalize on students' interests and relevance to their everyday lives heighten their learning (Chugani, 1998; Pawlak, Magarinos, Melchor, McEwen, & Strickland, 2003).

Finally, let's remember that many students find great joy in taking fitness and fine arts classes. For some students, these classes are the reason they show up at school each day and give them motivation to persevere in their other courses. Thus, eliminating such courses not only prevents some students from experiencing joyful learning but also thwarts students' academic growth.

ELLs, like other students, use the learning opportunities afforded by recess, PE, and fine arts classes to expand their content-area academic vocabulary. Recess, in particular, is also a time to socialize and provides an opportunity for these students to further develop basic interpersonal communicative skills (BICS), the language skills they need to interact socially with their peers.

Although we believe that focusing on the cognitive side of learning is important, there should still be room for thinking about learning as a pleasurable experience (i.e., the noncognitive side of learning) and how to create a context that will promote such pleasure. Like Olson (2009), we find this lack of focus on pleasurable learning (*joyful learning*) troubling because "pleasure in learning is one of the transcendent experiences of human life, one that offers meaning and a sense of connection in ways that few other activities can" (p. 30). But how can we attend to the pleasure that can be found in learning—or immerse our students in the joy of learning? Will attending to joy better ensure that students' learning of specific content has staying power? In this chapter we answer these important questions.

## Defining Joyful Learning

We define *joyful learning* as acquiring knowledge or skills in ways that cause pleasure and happiness. Recently the focus has been on the first half of that definition (e.g., knowledge or skills) to the exclusion of the second half (e.g., pleasure and happiness). The joyful learning environment does not necessarily equate to an "anything goes" or a chaotic atmosphere. Instead, what we are suggesting is that wrestling with new ideas and taking risks to learn new content requires persistence and the willingness to work through difficulties as they arise; through this experience, students experience joyful learning. Joyful learning is in keeping with what Waterman (2005) called "high effort-liked activities." As Tough (2012) substantiated, learning takes grit—and joy emanates from the pursuit of attaining new learning as much or more so than attaining it. Tough's point echoes that of Rantala and Maatta (2012), whose ethnographic and observational research led them to conclude that engaging in the activity is what produced students' pleasure and joy.

## A Joyful Learning Framework

Our review of the research and reflection on our own experiences have helped us see that joy has *everything* to do with learning. What also became clear to us is that understanding why joyful learning is so important left questions about how to implement it unanswered. We saw the need to create a framework that would help teachers make decisions about joyful learning more systematic, intentional, and purposeful. Our framework consists of three parts.

1. Five motivational generalizations: adaptive self-efficacy and competence beliefs, adaptive attributions and beliefs about control, higher levels of interest and intrinsic motivation, higher levels of value, and goals. These generalizations are shown in Figure 1.1.

2. Five elements that need to be assessed and evaluated in order to get the most from joyful learning: learners, teachers, texts and materials, assessments, and schoolwide configurations.

3. Five key areas to promote joyful learning: school community, physical environment, whole-group instruction, small-group instruction, and individual instruction.

As a practical extension of joyful learning, we have also identified teaching activities in each of the five areas that are compatible with what we learned. We offer those activities (in Chapter 3) so that you can see how the

FIGURE 1.1
**Generalizations About Motivation, and Instructional Implications**

| Generalization | Description | Instructional Implication |
|---|---|---|
| Adaptive self-efficacy and competence beliefs motivate students. | *Self-efficacy* focuses on judgment about one's ability to successfully perform a general task ("I'm good at math") or a specific given task ("I'm very good at solving story problems"). *Competence* beliefs focus on how well a person expects to perform ("I can do this"). | • Provide clear and accurate feedback regarding self-efficacy and competence, and focus on students' developing competence, expertise, and skill.<br>• Design tasks that challenge students yet provide opportunities for success.<br>• Involve students in monitoring their progress and growth so they can discover insights about themselves as learners. |
| Adaptive attributions and control beliefs motivate students. | *Attributions* and *control beliefs* are beliefs about what might cause success or failure with a given task and the degree of control one has over attaining the learning at hand. For example, "If I think deeper about this and make a greater effort, I will be able to do this" versus "I'm not as lucky as my friend who got this right." | • Provide feedback that emphasizes learning process, including the importance of effort, strategies, and self-control.<br>• Provide strategy instruction that goes beyond declarative knowledge (what) and includes procedural (how) and conditional (why and when) knowledge as well.<br>• Use language that focuses on controllable aspects of learning (effort, ways of thinking, strategy knowledge) and redirect language that focuses on uncontrollable aspects (luck, genes, other people's behavior)<br>• Share examples of how "failure" is a natural part of the ultimate successful efforts. Let learners know "if at first you don't succeed, join the club!" |
| Higher levels of interest and intrinsic motivation motivate students. | *Value* is the importance that an individual associates with a task. *Intrinsic value* (see Wigfield & Eccles, 2002) is the enjoyment or interest the learner experiences when completing a given activity ("I can't wait to find the time so I can finish reading the next book in this series"). | • Use assessment surveys that allow for insights about and across students in terms of their interests in topics, learning methods, and materials.<br>• Provide stimulating and interesting activities that incorporate many different materials.<br>• Provide a variety of activities, some of which are unique.<br>• Provide content and tasks that are meaningful to students.<br>• Show interest and involvement in the content and activities.<br>• Allow for choice in the selection of activities, content, and materials. |

| Generalization | Description | Instructional Implication |
|---|---|---|
| Higher levels of value motivate students. | Other forms of value are attainment, utility, and cost (Wigfield & Eccles, 2002). *Attainment* is the importance the learner attaches to doing well on the task. *Utility* is how useful the task is to achieving a future goal ("I want to do well on this essay because I want to post it on the school website"). *Cost* is perception of the activity in terms of time and effort ("This will be a helpful way to review and it won't take a bunch of time"). | • Use assessment surveys that allow for insights about and across students in terms of short-term goals, long-term goals, and current behaviors related to school work.<br>• Provide tasks, material, and activities that are relevant and useful to students and allow for some personal identification.<br>• Discuss with students the importance and utility of the content they are learning and the activities they complete. Help them understand why they are doing what they are doing. |
| Goals motivate and direct students. | *Goal content*, which focuses on establishing something to attain, and *goal orientation*, which focuses on the purpose or reason for engaging in an activity, are two important parts to consider when thinking about goals. *Mastery goal orientation* encourages students to approach the task in order to learn it well and gain new competence. *Performance goal orientation* leads one to demonstrate ability for others to seek reward or recognition (Rueda, 2011). | • Use organizational and management structures that encourage personal and social responsibility, including the setting of personal and classwide goals.<br>• Provide a safe, comfortable, and predictable environment.<br>• Use cooperative and collaborative groups to afford students with opportunities to attain both social and academic goals.<br>• Discuss with students the importance of mastering learning and understanding course and lesson content.<br>• Use task, reward, and evaluation structures that promote mastery, learning, effort, progress, and self-improvement standards and deemphasize social comparison or norm-referenced standards. |

Generalizations adapted from Pintrich, 2003.

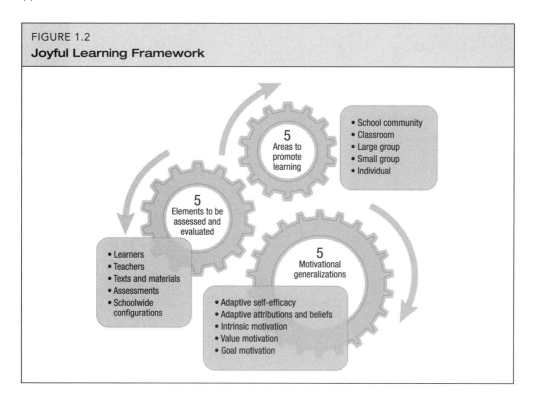

FIGURE 1.2
**Joyful Learning Framework**

framework comes to life in a classroom. The full framework for joyful learning appears in Figure 1.2 and is the basis for planning and teaching and learning using our research and experience.

## Setting Up Joyful Learning Experiences

Pleasure and joy are synonymous and truly can be found in learning environments. Olson (2009) noted that there are three kinds of pleasure that prompt learning: autonomous pleasure, social reward, and tension and release. Although often overlooked, autonomous pleasure has a sizeable effect on attitude and performance; we can't overemphasize the role that choice plays in joyful learning. When summarizing research related to autonomy, Pink (2009) concluded, "Autonomy promotes greater conceptual understanding, better grades, enhanced persistence at school and in sports activities, higher productivity, less burnout, and greater levels of psychological well-being" (p. 89). The three pleasures (autonomous, social reward, and tension and release) together suggest that joyful learning encompasses motivation and engagement. Here we'll discuss what motivation and engagement mean to teachers seeking to establish a joyful learning environment.

## Motivation

Finding ways to motivate children is not difficult. But motivating them to learn sets up an additional challenge, and motivating students to learn in school complicates that challenge. As Pressley (2006) pointed out

> Academic motivation is a fragile commodity. . . . For academic motivation to remain high, students must be successful and perceive that they are successful. . . . The policies of most elementary schools are such that most students will experience declining motivation, perceiving that they are not doing well, at least compared to other students. (p. 372)

The good news is the wealth of research about what motivates students to learn in classrooms. As Pressley stated, "much is being learned about how to reengineer schools so that high academic motivation is maintained" (2006, p. 372). Most relevant to our discussion is that researchers (e.g., Ames, 1992; Bandura, 1997; Deci & Ryan, 1985; Dweck, 2009; Locke & Latham, 2002; Wigfield & Eccles, 2002) have created many different social-cognitive models and constructs in an effort to answer and explain how to best motivate students. According to Pintrich (2003), regardless of the model or construct, all can be classified into one of five motivational generalizations, each of which has instructional implications (refer to Figure 1.1).

Teachers who understand and use motivation principles may be better equipped to discover ways to construct joyful learning experiences. But as Pintrich (2003) cautioned, when considering how to best capitalize on these motivation principles to create joyful learning experiences, there is no one-size-fits-all model. Rather, paying attention to what motivates their particular students will lead teachers to design motivational classrooms including activities that students perceive to be fun as a way to motivate them and spark their learning.

Many different combinations of motivation principles are viable. As Dolezal, Welsh, Pressley, and Vincent (2003) discovered, teachers who highly engage their students use many different motivating practices, including engaging them with activities that require high effort. Guthrie (2011) echoed this in noting that "motivation is diverse" (p. 177); it is multifaceted and complex, developmental, and situational, varies across different classroom contexts, and is affected by personal and social variables (Guthrie & Wigfield, 1997). A single approach to motivate all learners should be questioned as much as using a single instructional technique to teach all learners. Remember

- Any single approach has strengths and weaknesses.
- Exclusive use of any one approach magnifies its weaknesses.
- Exclusive use privileges some learners but not all.
- Single approaches fail to account for changes in motivation factors over time.
- Mandated single approaches disarm teachers from being adequately equipped to motivate all students who happen to be their responsibility in any given school year.

In other words, anyone who thinks there's one right way to motivate learners has probably never worked with more than one child.

Consider these three examples, from Cushman's *Fires in the Mind: What Kids Can Tell Us About Motivation and Mastery* (2010, p. 100). After reading each, take another look at Figure 1.1 (pp. 12–13) and identify which principle or principles each exemplifies.

*The science teacher:* "He'd have us all stand up and pretend to be molecules, like actually act out what their jobs are—cell organelles, nucleus and mitochondria, and stuff like that. That definitely stuck in my head." Chelsea.

*The language arts teacher:* "We had to work in groups and put on a play for the class. Everyone in the group had to contribute something to the play and work cohesively. I'm not that great of an actress but I enjoyed it, even though I was a little shy. It came out great." Iona

*The art teacher*: 'We chose to take a picture together of our faces and make a mosaic. It was a very long process and we were so new at it that we learned more than just making a mosaic. After a while we got the hang of it and it was really fun. Once we got really good at it, our teacher took us to a museum to look at mosaics and we were fascinated with them." Bianca

So, how do we attend to joyful learning? Making sure that students are motivated is a logical starting place. However, not all of the strategies teachers use to motivate students lead to joy. When motivation to learn is structured around compliance values or extrinsic rewards, actual joy from learning can remain a bit elusive or transitory (Kohn, 1999).

The question, then, becomes how we can gauge the level of students' motivation. Are there ways to make what is often covert more overt? Considering student engagement can help us answer this important question.

## Engagement

Closely related to motivation, *engagement* indicates that the learner is involved and immersed in an activity. Wlodkowski and Ginsberg (1995) defined engagement as the visible outcome of motivation, the natural capacity to direct energy in the pursuit of a goal. It usually includes three conditions: learners can sense that success is within their reach (*self-efficacy*), they value the outcome (*valuing*) from the activity, and they feel safe in contexts in which the learning is taking place (*environments*) (Brophy, 2008).

Engagement also can serve to mediate other learning and achievement. According to Pressley and colleagues (2001), exemplary teachers who taught students with similar demographics and also had high levels of classroom engagement were able to have a

Providing an engaging, collaborative, and safe environment can lower students' affective filters. As Krashen (1987) noted, low motivation, low self-esteem, and anxiety can raise the affective filter and impede language acquisition. Using instructional strategies that build collaboration, engagement, and a safe classroom environment assist in lowering students' affective filters and simultaneously enhance their motivation and language acquisition.

more significant impact on traditional performance and achievement. In those classrooms, 90 percent of students were on task 90 percent of the time. And who better to judge engagement than the classroom teacher? Although most are able to note whether students are engaged, better understanding of engagement enables teachers to look more in-depth and get more out of their observations. To better understand engagement, we offer the following four points:

1. Engagement has four essential components. When students are engaged, they are attentive, are committed, are persistent, and attribute value to their work.

2. Entertainment and engagement are different.

3. Engage learners using behavioral, cognitive, and noncognitive strategies.

4. Engagement should be determined by talking with and listening to students.

Schlechty (2011) noted that engaged students are attentive, committed, persistent, and meaning seekers. What does this look like in the classroom?

• *Attentive* learners pay attention to the task at hand and stay focused on it.

• *Committed* learners voluntarily (without any extrinsic reward or threat of punishment for not engaging) participate in a task using all available time, effort, and attention to complete it.

• *Persistent* learners stick with a task even when it gets difficult.

• *Meaning seekers* find value in the tasks that are associated with the work they are to accomplish.

Understanding these components of engagement helps prevent being fooled by students' behavior. For instance, a glance around the room might indicate that all students are engaged with a given activity. Upon closer inspection, however, we might discover that some students are on task but are not engaged in terms of the four components. Students who are on task might mindlessly complete an activity just to get it finished and to be compliant, yet a close examination of their work offers evidence that they were anything but engaged: many of the problems might be left blank (lacking persistence), and those that are answered make little sense (lacking effort to make meaning). Clearly, engagement is much more than simply being on task.

The difference between entertainment and engagement is fairly clear just by thinking about the two words. We all know that it is fairly easy to entertain students (remember the Friday afternoon video?), but engagement is a significantly different challenge. Katz and Chard (2000) reminded us that engagement involves getting students interested in the world in which they live. If students become interested in their environment, they will always be able to find something to keep them interested in life. In contrast, we often seek entertainment to distract us from our daily lives. We are diverted from paying attention to important matters, and that distraction can lead us away from reaching our goals. In the end, entertainment is fairly transitory and doesn't last long. Waterman (2005) made a similar distinction in describing low effort, high-liked activities (entertainment) and high effort-liked activities (engagement).

Sometimes it is necessary for teachers to provide students with additional scaffolding and support to assist their meaning seeking, especially if the student is not able to independently comprehend the language. Offering visuals, exaggerating gestures, building background knowledge, and developing vocabulary are ways to support students at all levels of comprehension in their meaning-seeking quest.

As teachers, our job is to engage students, not to entertain them. We get them involved by providing students with tasks that enable them to be attentive, committed, and persistent meaning seekers who find a pleasure in learning that is more sustaining and longer lasting than efforts to entertain. Said another way, "Students who are engaged do not need to be entertained. They and their teachers are getting too much joy out of what they are doing and they are having fun while they are doing it" (Schlechty, 2011, p. 26).

Does this mean that we should forgo dressing up as a specific story character or historical figure to deliver content? Should we never use humor, tell a funny story, or smile? Absolutely not! How unfortunate if we were to abandon any or all techniques we use because we know our students and know that using such entertainment devices will lead to their engagement. Fun is also a way for students to build social relationships, to build community (Rantala & Maatta, 2012). What we're suggesting instead is mindful, purposeful use of each—understanding why we are doing what we are doing and how entertainment and engagement contribute to the larger picture. Entertaining becomes a means, not an end. Like the poet who is forced to economize on words to convey a powerful message, so, too, must the teacher use props, humor, and other activities students deem to be fun in purposeful, economical ways.

Engage learners using behavioral, cognitive, and affective strategies. This is actually a relatively new concept that researchers continue to explore and define. Fredericks, Blumenfeld, and Paris (2004) suggested three different types of engagement:

- *Behavioral*, in which the learner actively performs activities.
- *Cognitive*, in which the learner uses thinking strategies to learn content.
- *Affective*, in which the learner expresses enjoyment about learning.

Much of the research on engagement has focused on the behavioral aspects of engagement. The cognitive and noncognitive aspects of engagement are only starting to get attention. These aspects are particularly important to us when we seek to share joy in learning with our students.

Talking with and listening to students is a critical part of assessing engagement. They can offer information that cannot be gleaned from other sources, including details about their own learning that can help us to better understand our teaching. An added benefit of talking with students is that it helps them better understand themselves. If students are provided with an opportunity to talk about their perceptions of their level of engagement and the factors that contributed to their engagement (or lack thereof), they become self-aware—and as a result are in a better position to either keep or modify their perceptions. Change begins with awareness.

Therefore, making time to talk with students is anything but an option if we truly want to know their level of engagement. Here are four questions that you can use to elicit information from students:

1. On a scale of 1 to 5 (5 is highest), rate how much you enjoyed class today. Give a reason for the rating.

2. If you came to any difficult parts of learning, what did you do to work through them?

3. Why do you think you were expected to do the activities in class? Do you think they helped you learn what you were supposed to learn?

4. What other activities or strategies do you want me to include in the lesson? Why?

Questions similar to these can be a part of informal conversations, or they might be catalysts for a more formal conversation. One way to engage all students is to use these different questions one at a time over a period of time, perhaps as an exit slip to conclude a lesson. The point is to use information gleaned from the students to look for patterns across the class to determine how to adjust instruction. For example, in response to the first question, students might indicate that what made the class enjoyable was the opportunity to work collaboratively with others on a topic that they as a group chose to investigate; the teacher could use this information to structure future lessons.

## Reasons to Implement Joyful Learning

Joy is an integral part of learning, with staying power. Joy leads students to learning rather than away from it.

**Joy capitalizes on what we know about how to best motivate students.** Motivation is multifaceted and there are many variables to consider. And we need to thoughtfully use these options as we discover how to create physical environments and classroom climates that foster students' desire to learn. We can intentionally design whole-group, small-group, and independent work for and with the students themselves. If students are to be motivated to complete a task, they need to see the importance behind it. As Cushman (2010) stressed, "If kids do not think a task is important, they will not want to do it, even if they could do it perfectly. And if they do not expect that they can succeed at a task, they also lose desire to try" (p. 54).

**Joy enables us to build on what we know about engagement.** In the broadest views of engagement, learners are active and get a sense of joy from the learning in which they are engaged because it is meaningful to them. They are pursuing what Waterman (2005) called "high effort-liked activities" (p. 165). They understand why they are doing what they are doing, and consequently see value in what they are doing. As the student Micha said,

> You want to delve into the reason why you are doing something, instead of just blindly following what the teacher tells you to do. If you are getting the answer without really realizing why it's important, it's empty. You are not really learning. You are going to drop that later, because it has no importance to you in your life. (Cushman, 2010, p. 8)

Engaged learners delve deeper into what they are learning rather than skim the surface. They are far more interested in conceptual understanding than recalling facts. A sense of joy emanates, as students are actively involved in seeking out information related to a meaningful topic.

**Joy enables us to focus on the whole child.** One of the major tenets of the Whole Child Initiative is that educators must go beyond academic achievement when considering the full scope of learning. In order to be a successful learner, one needs to be "knowledgeable, emotionally and physically healthy, civically inspired, engaged in the arts, prepared for work and economic self-sufficiency, and ready for the world beyond formal schooling" (ASCD, 2007, p. 4). One way to develop such learners is to think of the *whole child* as one who embraces many attributes, including being intellectually active, creative and curious, empathetic, kind, caring, and fair, as well as being a critical thinker. Beyond the intellectual stimulation that leads one to joyful learning, students need to feel safe to take the necessary risks associated with new learning. They need to feel cared for and valued. All of these attributes contribute to joyful learning. We do a disservice to the academic (cognitive) aspects of learning when we ignore these noncognitive, affective dimensions. Attention to the latter can help us more effectively address the former.

**Joy acknowledges that the learner is influenced by the contexts in which learning takes place.** As we discuss joyful learning, we must remember that teaching and learning do not take place in a vacuum. As Rueda (2011) reminded us, "The sociocultural context can influence motivation in a variety of ways" (p. 46). He observed that contexts are not neutral; they place learners in interactive situations in which what an individual knows is often shaped by what is new in the context. Complex social and cultural contexts—forces within and beyond the classroom—end up contributing to the identity of the learner. Considering how these forces influence how learners see themselves as readers, writers, scientists, historians, or mathematicians is critical. Learners' identities are also formed by how they want to be seen by others, and by how they are seen by others in these contexts. In the end, the learner's identity, which is often based on perceptions, contributes to what one can or cannot do as a learner (Hall, 2009).

So, how do we know that students are motivated? Making sure that they are engaged is a logical answer. How do we know if they are engaged? We watch them, looking to verify that they are attentive, committed, persistent, and attribute value to their work. We talk with them about their level of engagement and listen to their voices. We take a look at the products students produce and attend to how they share them. We must think about engagement more broadly. If our only way of thinking about engagement is by looking through the lens of on-task behaviors, we can see that students can be engaged, but we might not see a level of joy. We need to remember that when students are engaged, they enjoy what they are doing.

# CHAPTER 2

# Assessing and Evaluating Joyful Learning

Fast-forward two weeks: Mike, Mary, and Kathy meet to discuss what they are learning about how to help students rediscover the joy of learning. Kathy begins by saying, "I've been doing a lot of thinking about how to help my students enjoy learning, and I've realized that there are so many different things to consider. For one thing, I need to take a good look at myself; I'm not sure whether my passion and enjoyment for teaching come through to my students."

Mary exclaims, "I wondered the same thing about myself! In fact, I got to thinking that maybe the reason that my students resist writing so much is that I haven't given them enough control over the process. Sometimes we set the conferencing schedule, and then I'm frustrated because some students are not prepared to conference. Maybe I should let students set the conference schedule—you know, sign up when they are ready."

Mike nods. "I've been thinking about the materials I use as a part of my lessons. Maybe the reason my kids don't seem to enjoy social studies is that I am the only one selecting texts. Maybe I should let them do some choosing and hold them accountable for what they choose."

As their conversation shows, Kathy, Mike, and Mary have shifted their focus from learners to the elements extending beyond learners that foster joyful learning, and the complexity of addressing all of these. These educators have reached the point where a systematic assessment (i.e., asking questions and the process used to obtain answers) and evaluation (i.e., interpreting the gathered evidence) of key elements (i.e., learners, teachers, texts and materials, assessments, and schoolwide configurations) could help them target specific concerns. In this chapter, we discuss how to assess and evaluate these factors, to help answer the question of what teachers need to know to maximize joyful learning.

## Element 1: Assessing and Evaluating Learners

It's essential to look at your learners to identify where they are and what they need to become more joyful learners. If we don't know how joyful learners are to begin with, how can we understand how to maximize their joyful learning?

As our previous discussion about motivation and engagement and this chapter's opening vignette make clear, assessing and evaluating the affective outcomes that contribute to joyful learning is complicated. Affective outcomes such as motivation are not easily defined because they are multifaceted and complex (Guthrie & Wigfield, 1997).

A review of the research in motivation shows 17 potential affective outcomes for learners that impact motivation, engagement, and joyful learning. When assessing learners, we need to consider and evaluate these dimensions: learner identity, belief in general abilities, belief in the ability to complete specific tasks, degree of expectation for success, degree of curiosity, desire for recognition from others, desire to comply with others, ability to stay involved with learning, attraction to challenge, the importance of learning, competition against self and others, value of social involvement, personal interests, sense of locus of control, internalized reasons to engage self in task, self-regulating behaviors, and prosocial behaviors (Pugh, personal communication, October 2012).

Each dimension may not warrant individual attention, and it should be noted that some of them combine to foster critical outcomes. For example, as we discussed in Chapter 1, engagement often results from a

Language barriers can affect ELLs' perceptions about their expectations for success. Their beliefs about their ability as learners in their first language might vary greatly from the classroom setting, where they are still acquiring English. This is also true for students with other learning challenges.

combination of expecting success, seeing the outcome as important, and feeling safe in the learning environment. Trying to focus on both a large number of outcomes and individual learners can be daunting; we advocate instead narrowing the focus initially to a more manageable number.

## Essential Questions

For each affective dimension, there are key questions teachers should ask, a continuum for evaluating students, and instructional implications. Three essential questions should guide any assessment of and response to learners' thinking, desires, and knowledge (see Figure 2.1):

**Do learners think they can succeed?** This question focuses on students' identities as learners. How do they see themselves? How do they view their abilities? Do they feel capable of undertaking specific content-area tasks?

**Why do learners want to succeed?** This question addresses aspects of learner motivation. When considering how to engage students in joyful learning, it's essential to understand what motivates them. Is it recognition? A challenge? Competition? Understanding motivation can help identify ways to help students value learning.

**Do learners know what they need to do to succeed?** This question focuses on students' self-knowledge—and what they believe is necessary for success in learning. To what extent do students believe they can control learning? What individual reasons do they have to stay engaged with learning? Do they exhibit behaviors that will enhance and assist them in this pursuit?

## Beyond the Learner

Although the assessment and evaluation begins with a focus on the learner, it cannot end there. Affective outcomes are neither inherent to nor

FIGURE 2.1
## Assessing and Evaluating Learners

| Affective Dimension | Questions to Guide Assessment | Special Considerations |
|---|---|---|
| | *Do learners think they can succeed?* | |
| Identity | How do students see themselves as learners?<br><br>*weak identity* ———— *strong identity* | Remember that some subject areas are fairly broad-based and represent multiple disciplines within a content area. |
| Self-efficacy: General | How do students think they perform in school generally and in each content area specifically?<br><br>*helpless* ———— *confident* | Self-efficacy is based primarily on the learner's perception. Whether learners view themselves as capable or incapable can matter more than true capability in a subject or school in general. |
| Self-efficacy: Specific | How do students think they will perform specific tasks required in school?<br><br>*helpless* ———— *confident* | Efficacy also can operate at a specific-task level. Learners may feel capable in one aspect of the instruction (discussions, projects) but less so in another aspect of instruction (labs, tests). |
| Expectation of success | Do students expect they have the potential for success generally and specifically in the learning activities on which they will be working?<br><br>*anticipate failure* ———— *expect success* | Instruction needs to be structured so that the learner envisions success within reach. It's not just about the learner having success; it's about having success that the learner will see as meaningful. Making something easy will not have the same impact as structuring instruction so that more difficult tasks are achievable. |
| | *Why do learners want to succeed?* | |
| Curiosity | What is the student's level of curiosity about learning in general and specifically in given content areas?<br><br>*indifferent* ———— *inquisitive* | In content areas that are more process oriented (reading and writing), value might come from being a means to learn more about a content area. For example, a student might get motivated about reading because it can be used to satisfy curiosity about things in science. |

*(continued on next page)*

FIGURE 2.1

## Assessing and Evaluating Learners (continued)

| Affective Dimension | Questions to Guide Assessment | Special Considerations |
| --- | --- | --- |
| Recognition | Do students seek to have others see them as learners generally, and more specifically as students in given content areas?<br><br>avoid — seek | Recognition by others varies for different learners. For many, it's how they want to be perceived by peers. For some, it might be how they want to be perceived by their families or even school staff members. |
| Compliance | Do students perceive a reason for generally engaging in learning or specifically engaging in the content area, even if they don't want to?<br><br>resistant — compliant | Many learners think specific tasks and classes are "boring" but complete the work anyway because they see some reason for compliance. Remember that compliance, although motivating, may not always lead to joyous efforts. |
| Involvement | How involved are students with a learning experience?<br><br>disengaged — engaged | Involvement usually implies desire or even passion. The learner really likes to get lost in the learning activity related to the subject area. |
| Challenge | How do students react to the level of challenge provided by learning experiences in general and those in specific content areas?<br><br>avoid — embrace | Generally, learners who seek challenge are more motivated when they find it—though increasingly some learners react to challenging situations by resisting. For this reason, challenge often needs to be balanced by an expectation of success. |
| Importance | When compared to other priorities competing for students' attention, where do they place learning experiences in general and those in specific content areas?<br><br>low priority — high priority | For some students, it's not a lack of skill or even a lack of interest in the subject area; it's just that the subject area ranks low on a list of priorities. In school settings, different subject areas also have to compete against each other. |

| | | |
|---|---|---|
| Competition | How motivated are students by competition, in general and in specific content areas?<br><br>noncompetitive — competitive | Competition can motivate some students but may have the opposite effect on other students. Competition should work better if learners are contributing to group goals or if they are competing against personal goals. Pitting students against each other may be less successful as a motivational tool. |
| Social | Which types of social instruction influence students' performance in general and in specific content areas?<br><br>individual — group | For many students, learning needs to be relational. This means more than just having students work together or discuss with one another; it means creating instruction that helps students develop relationships over time. |
| Personal interest | Do students take a personal interest in learning?<br><br>bored — interested | Learners come into classrooms with specific interests on which teachers can capitalize, but teachers can also create interest in the learning situation. |
| *Do learners know what they need to do to succeed?* | | |
| Locus of control | To what factors do students attribute their success or lack of it?<br><br>external — internal | When learners perceive an internal locus of control, they attribute their success to effort they make. Learners who attribute their success to external factors such as luck, innate ability, or the teacher may become convinced that effort doesn't have much to do with success. |
| Internalized motivation | What type of influences or reasons motivate students?<br><br>extrinsic — intrinsic | Some students have intrinsic reasons to engage in learning, and our main responsibility as teachers is to stay out of their way and let them pursue their desires. Adding external reasons to engage in a task can actually diminish the value of the task for some learners. |
| Self-regulating behaviors | How well are my students able to work independently?<br><br>controlled — autonomous | Learning opportunities often require the ability to work and learn without specific guidance from the teacher. |
| Positive social goals | To what degree do my other goals contribute to prosocial behaviors in my learners (e.g., attendance, punctuality, preparedness, leadership, interaction)?<br><br>low — high | In order for learning to take place, students need to show up, show up on time, and show up prepared. They can contribute to a more conducive learning climate by showing positive leadership and interactions with others. Behaviors like these can be reflective of motivated learners; problems with these types of interactions may result from a lack of motivation. |

solely the responsibility of the learner. It is essential to also assess and evaluate the effects of teachers, texts and materials, assessments, and schoolwide configurations on student learning. The same affective dimension categories that help us assess and evaluate learners can and should provide the basis for considering and assessing these additional elements.

## Element 2: Assessing and Evaluating Ourselves as Teachers

We have often heard teachers lament, "These kids aren't motivated." This comment suggests that motivation is solely the responsibility of the learner. When Tatum said "Folks, if they are showing up every day, you have to teach them" (2009) he was saying that if students are not motivated, it is the teacher's responsibility to motivate them. Motivation is integral to, rather than separate from, effective instruction. A teacher can't be satisfied with planning and teaching a "great" lesson if it falls short because learners are not motivated or engaged. Exemplary teachers who have a high impact on students by traditional performance and achievement measures are intentional in addressing motivation (Allington & Johnston, 2002; Pressley et al., 2001).

### Understanding Affective Outcomes

Joyful learning results from an intentional effort to address the wide variety of factors that influence affective outcomes (Tough, 2012; Waterman, 2005). Affective, noncognitive outcomes

• Vary across classroom contexts, subject areas, topics within subject areas, or even tasks within subject areas.

• Vary across developmental levels. What works for younger learners might not work when they become older. And because kids vary even within developmental levels, their variance further complicates addressing affective outcomes (Fiedler, 2012).

• Vary by personal and social influences. Understanding this may shed some light on why some learners find more joy in certain classroom settings (e.g., working by themselves) than others (working in a small group).

Like cognitive outcomes, affective outcomes are influenced by a variety of factors—many of which are controlled by the teacher (Farrington et al., 2012). Because successful outcomes for students are primarily a result of adult (i.e., teacher) interaction with students (Cambourne, 1995, 2001), when seeking to create a joyful learning environment, any analysis of affective outcomes needs to address variables controlled by teachers.

## Essential Questions

In evaluating your own effect as a teacher on students' identities as learners, consider how your identity as a learner affects your teaching. As teachers, we are learners; the questions that we ask about our students' engagement and motivation provide a basis for us to reflect on our own learning and teaching.

**Do learners think they can succeed?** Do you believe in your general and specific abilities as a learner? What do you do to promote your students' confidence in their abilities? How do you model your own expectations for success and help improve your students' expectations?

**Why do learners want to succeed?** What causes you to want to succeed as a learner? How do you help your students want to succeed? How can you respond to the varying motivations of your students (such as curiosity, recognition, and competition) to help them value learning?

**Do learners know what they need to do to succeed?** How well do you model internal locus of control, internalized motivations, self-regulating behaviors, and positive social behaviors? How well do you help them develop these skills that support self-directed learning?

# Element 3: Assessing and Evaluating Texts and Materials

The texts and materials students use in the classroom also influence joyful learning. When considering which texts to use and how to use them in classroom settings, consider what type of effect they will have on the learners. Sometimes teachers control decisions about texts and materials, and other times these decisions are mandated by the state, school district, or school administration. Sometimes availability and quantity determine how you use the materials in class. Regardless of who makes the decision, it is important to be aware that learners glean something from all classroom materials. Students are never *not* learning from a text . . . even if they are only learning that they do not want to engage with the text.

## Learner Interaction with Text and Materials

If we think about texts in the broadest sense, learners are always "reading" something (Shannon, 2012). What they are reading, viewing, or listening to sends messages to them, and these messages can and do have affective outcomes. Sometimes the messages are intentional, but other times the material itself sends messages to students. For example, complex leveled reading systems may unintentionally send messages to students about their perceived reading levels; for students' self-efficacy, levels define who they are as learners.

Grouping ELLs and choosing texts and materials solely based on the fact that they speak more than one language can send mixed messages about perceived learning levels and affect student self-efficacy. Alternative language groupings may be by needs, comprehension strategies, interests, or self-selection.

A learner's interaction with texts and materials is quite complex. Language-based processes (i.e., reading, viewing, listening, speaking, and writing) are interactive because language users bring their background and construct meanings as they interpret the authors' messages. Therefore, messages intended by authors and producers are anything but stable as different learners construct meanings based on their prior knowledge and personal experiences and background.

## Essential Questions

When choosing or evaluating texts and materials, consider how they will affect students' identities as learners:

**Do learners think they can succeed?** Do the texts and materials you use help improve learners' identities? Do they encourage and support students' confidence in their general and specific abilities and enhance expectations for success?

**Why do learners want to succeed?** How do the text and materials you use help students want to succeed? Do they foster motivation and help your students value learning?

**Do learners know what they need to do to succeed?** Do the text and materials you use help students develop an internal locus of control and internalized reasons to stay engaged in tasks? Do the materials promote students' acquisition of self-regulating and positive social behaviors?

## Element 4: Assessing and Evaluating Assessments

In many ways, assessments are another type of text or set of materials, so when selecting and using assessment tools in classroom settings, we need to consider how they will affect students. Although teachers often develop tests and quizzes to use in their own classrooms, many of the assessments are selected by school administrators, districts, and state boards of education. Regardless of the extent of control over decision making, when seeking to develop a joyful learning environment, it's important to evaluate the effect of assessments.

### Assessing Affective Outcomes

Two important issues surface when examining assessments within the context of joyful learning. First, there is the issue of what we are *not* assessing. Although assessing affective outcomes involves comprehensive observations and ongoing monitoring of learners (i.e., formative assessment), because affective outcomes have garnered less attention than cognitive outcomes, appropriate assessments may be less available and less familiar to teachers who are familiar (and thus more comfortable) with cognitive assessment techniques. Our own experiences have taught us that what is assessed receives the most instructional attention. To move toward joyful learning, we must give serious attention to affective outcomes—and what better way to do so than to assess them?

The second issue relates to what we are assessing. *Joy* and *testing* are two words we don't often see in the same sentence. In an era of increasing accountability, the time, energy, and resources devoted to assessment have begun to dominate the school experience—often to the detriment of joyful learning experiences. Instead of enjoying award-winning books during reading instruction, students often encounter excerpts from them on standardized tests (Rowan, Correnti, Miller, & Camburn, 2009). Fostering joy in reading wonderful books is significantly different from trying to foster joy from reading an excerpt on a test.

## Essential Questions

It's not just the experience of testing that can detract from joyful learning; the results themselves also have an effect on learners' sense of self and their growth. Using test results often leads to public decisions about labeling, sorting, classifying, and placing students—all of which affect students' affective outcomes.

**Do learners think they can succeed?** How do the assessments that students experience help improve their identities as learners? Can the results from the assessments provide insight about students' confidence in their abilities and expectations for success? Can the results from the assessments improve student identities as learners?

Standardized assessments often underestimate ELLs' academic progress and potential (Cummins & Sayers, 1995). Different sociolinguistic and cultural backgrounds and adjustments to new sociocultural settings can result in over-, under-, or misidentification of ELLs (Gonzalez, Brusca-Vega, & Yawkey, 1997; Klingner, J. K., et al., 2005). It is essential that teachers take into consideration language acquisition when assessing and referring students for special services.

**Why do learners want to succeed?** Do the assessments you use help identify students' motivations? Do the assessments appeal to these motivations and help students want to succeed? How can you use these assessments to help students value learning? How can you use the results of these assessments to help students value joyful learning?

**Do learners know what they need to do to succeed?** Do the assessments you use reveal results that can assist you in helping students develop an internal locus of control and internalized reasons to stay engaged in tasks? Do they assess students' self-regulating and social behaviors? Do they assess students' self-regulating and social behaviors critical for joyful learning?

# Element 5: Assessing and Evaluating Schoolwide Configurations

Although we applaud Kathy's, Mike's, and Mary's efforts to take control of their teaching and start a serious conversation about how to bring about joyful learning in their classrooms, joyful learning needs to be a schoolwide effort. As we have noted, although teachers control many of the decisions within their classrooms, others outside the classroom increasingly make many decisions about texts, materials, and assessments. Kathy, Mike, and Mary have to work within the real constraints of their school environment. A schoolwide effort, advantageous for teachers moving toward joyful learning, is even more important for learners.

Schoolwide conversations about joyful learning begin with examining the school's vision about what learning is and who learners are. A schoolwide vision that enhances joyful learning is broad and enables many students to see themselves as part of it. If a schoolwide recognition program consistently rewards a narrow group of learners, other students won't consider themselves part of that vision. At the other extreme, a recognition program that recognizes all (even when recognition may not be warranted) also diminishes the vision of the value of learning.

Schools can encourage the celebration of bilingual students as they think about how their schoolwide configurations help ELLs think they can succeed, want to succeed, and know what they need to succeed in this English-speaking setting. Celebrations can include bilingual presentations, family nights, and community events. Acknowledging the benefits of being bilingual and biliterate can be enhanced by introducing the school community to successful professionals who use more than one language in their work.

## Creating a Schoolwide Vision

From the moment we enter a school, we should be able to sense a vision of learning and learners that results in joyous efforts. Although teachers can create individual classroom environments to foster that result, those classrooms will work better in a school that fosters the same. Why should students' ability to experience joyful learning be dependent upon their classroom assignment?

Schoolwide conversations about joyful learning need to include an examination of the instructional methods promoted or required by the school administration. In addition to texts, materials, and assessments, instructional methods and programs affect classroom organization, group practices, and classroom discourse patterns. Programs that use classroom language as primarily a controlling, instrumental device (*regulatory*), for example, will lead students to different affective outcomes than programs that use classroom language as a probative, heuristic device (Halliday, 1975; Johnston, 2004, 2012).

## Essential Questions

Schoolwide conversations about joyful learning have the potential to bring educators together in a collaborative community, to look collectively at data, to develop potential plans for systematic change, and to communicate those plans to others. As when assessing the other elements that collectively affect joyful learning, assessing schoolwide configurations should be based on our three key questions about learners:

**Do learners think they can succeed?** How do schoolwide configurations, including classroom organization, grouping practices, and language discourse patterns, affect learners' identities, their confidence in their abilities, and their expectations of success? Does each individual classroom promote the schoolwide vision in helping learners believe they can succeed?

**Why do learners want to succeed?** How do schoolwide configurations impact learners' desire to succeed? Do they address a variety of learner motivations throughout the school and in individual classrooms?

**Do learners know what they need to do to succeed?** How do schoolwide configurations, including the physical environment, the use of whole-group activities, and individualized approaches to learning, affect students' internalized reasons to stay engaged in tasks, self-regulating behaviors, and positive social behaviors? Is there a schoolwide philosophy of management and instruction that leads everyone toward joyful learning (e.g., acts of kindness, tolerance, mindfulness, or awareness)?

## Assessing the Five Elements

To get the most from joyful learning, you must consider the five elements. Assessing and evaluating them must be guided by the key questions that keep the focus on the learner.

Still not sure where to begin? It's helpful to start by having conversations with supportive colleagues who share your interest in promoting joyful learning. Then focus on the element that interests you the most—whether learner, teacher, texts and materials, assessments, or schoolwide environment and configurations—and later expand to others. This process will help you evaluate not only your students but also the environment in which they learn.

We have developed two surveys to assist you in focusing on and assessing individual learners' joy and the factors that extend beyond learners; one instrument is designed for classroom use, and the other for a schoolwide assessment. The Affective Dimension Profile (p. 41) can help teachers assess how learner factors influence individual students' sense of joy. To better understand and help individual students, use the individual learner profile; understanding individual students' learner profiles can help you identify appropriate joyful learning instructional responses (see Figure 2.2). Creating a summary of individual learner profiles will give you a general picture of the pool of students in each classroom and help you see overall trends.

The Beyond Learners Survey (see pp. 44–45) can help teachers individually and collectively reflect on how teacher, texts and materials, assessments, and schoolwide configurations influence individual learners' sense of joy throughout the school day. Reflecting on each element will establish how well each is developed and being applied, and help identify those that might need to be enhanced (see Figure 2.3).

In Chapter 1, we presented the case for joyful learning. In this chapter, we provided what we need to know and how to systematically analyze joyful learning. In Chapter 3, we will move to applying these insights and ideas in practical ways as we ask and answer the next logical question: what do I do with this information?

| FIGURE 2.2 |
| --- |
| **Learner Profiles and Instructional Implications** |

| **For learners who . . .** | **Instructional implications/response** |
| --- | --- |
| Think they can succeed, want to succeed, and know what they need to do to succeed | Continue to provide engaging activities that capitalize on student interest and curiosity. |
| **For learners who have perceived difficulties with . . .** | **Instructional implications/response** |
| Wanting to succeed | Design instruction and activities that help students see the value in succeeding on given tasks. When they see how learning connects to their lives, students are more likely to want to succeed. |
| Thinking they can succeed | Focus on strengthening their identities and raising expectations. Many times the language we use with our students sends the best subtle messages to them that they are learners and can do this. |
| Knowing what they need to do to succeed | Focus on teaching explicit strategies that provide learners with what they need to move themselves forward. |
| Wanting to succeed *and* knowing what they need to do to succeed | Dig deeper into what they value and use that to bring purpose to instruction. Design lessons to make success strategies explicit. |
| Thinking they can succeed *and* knowing what they need to do to succeed | Use what motivates them to create opportunities that will lead to stronger identities (usually by learning more self-regulating strategies and behaviors). |
| Thinking they can succeed *and* desiring to succeed | If students know how to move themselves toward success, but just can't find value in doing that because they don't see themselves as one of "those," refocus attention on bringing the students back to insider status to help them see the value. |
| Thinking they can succeed, wanting to succeed, and knowing what they need to do to succeed | Almost anything we could do would help start to move these students in a new direction, but remember that joyful learning is an outcome of expectation and motivation and knowledge. Addressing just one area won't move these students forward. |

FIGURE 2.3

## Assessment Results and Suggested Activities for Improvement

| If assessment reveals ... | Suggested activities |
| --- | --- |
| Low scores on teacher or teachers' knowledge and ability to improve students' identities and confidence as learners, and to positively affect their motivation and ability to succeed | Use identity builders such as artifact displays (see p. 52).<br><br>Involve students in monitoring their progress and growth. Consider using questions such as those shown on page 21 in Chapter 1. |
| Low scores on texts and materials' enhancement of students' identities and confidence as learners, and positive effect on their motivation and ability to succeed | Actively involve all students in a whole-group activity in which each student can contribute to his own learning and that of others. (See the suggested activity on pp. 53–55.)<br><br>Consider using connected text sets (see pp. 57–58) to help students develop positive social behaviors while learning about a given topic. |
| Low scores on assessments as useful and supportive of students' identities and confidence as learners, and positive effect on student motivation and ability to succeed | Make sure your feedback to students emphasizes that learning is a process. Tell them how important effort, self-control, and application of strategies are to this process to attain a specific goal.<br><br>Use organizational and management structures (such as a focused readers workshop; see pp. 59–60) that encourage personal and social responsibility, including the setting of personal and classwide goals. |
| Low scores on schoolwide configurations as positively affecting students' identities and confidence as learners, and on student motivation and ability to succeed | Provide tasks, material, and activities that are relevant and useful to students and allow for some personal identification with school. Implement schoolwide projects such as Make a Difference (see pp. 50–51).<br><br>Provide a safe, comfortable, and predictable environment. Scheduling daily activities so that they occur at the same time every day is one way to provide this type of environment. |

## Affective Dimension Profiles

Complete an Affective Dimension Profile from your observations of each learner. For each affective dimension area, compute an overall score and note instructional implications under Areas of Strength or Need. Compile class results on the Classroom Affective Dimension Profile. Use the results to quickly remind you of the strengths and needs of each learner and overall classroom.

## Learner's Affective Dimension Profile

Learner: _____   Date: _____

| Dimension | Rating Scale | Areas of Strength or Need |
|---|---|---|
| *Do learners think they can succeed?* | | |
| Identity | Weak identity     Strong identity<br>1     2     3     4 | |
| Belief in general ability | Helpless     Competent<br>1     2     3     4 | |
| Belief in specific abilities | Helpless     Competent<br>1     2     3     4 | |
| Expectation of success | Avoids failure     Expects success<br>1     2     3     4 | |
| **Total score for this question:** _____**/16*** | | |
| *Why do learners want to succeed?* | | |
| Curiosity | Indifferent     Inquisitive<br>1     2     3     4 | |
| Recognition | Avoids     Seeks<br>1     2     3     4 | |
| Compliance | Resistant     Compliant<br>1     2     3     4 | |
| Involvement | Disengaged     Engaged<br>1     2     3     4 | |
| Challenge | Avoids     Embraces<br>1     2     3     4 | |
| Importance | Low priority     High priority<br>1     2     3     4 | |
| Competition | Noncompetitive     Competitive<br>1     2     3     4 | |
| Social interaction | Individual     Group<br>1     2     3     4 | |
| Personal interest | Bored     Interested<br>1     2     3     4 | |
| **Total score for this question:** _____**/36** | | |
| *Do learners know what they need to do to succeed?* | | |
| Locus of control | External     Internal<br>1     2     3     4 | |
| Reasons to engage self in task | Extrinsic     Intrinsic<br>1     2     3     4 | |
| Self-regulating behaviors | Controlled     Autonomous<br>1     2     3     4 | |
| Social behaviors | Antisocial     Prosocial<br>1     2     3     4 | |
| **Total score for this question:** _____**/16** | | |

## Classroom Affective Dimension Profile

**Class Period or Identification/Year** _____

| Learner | Do learners think they can succeed?   (16 possible*) | Why do learners want to succeed?   (36 possible**) | Do learners know what they need to do to succeed?   (16 possible*) |
|---------|---------|---------|---------|
| | __/16 | __/36 | __/16 |
| | __/16 | __/36 | __/16 |
| | __/16 | __/36 | __/16 |
| | __/16 | __/36 | __/16 |
| | __/16 | __/36 | __/16 |
| | __/16 | __/36 | __/16 |
| | __/16 | __/36 | __/16 |
| | __/16 | __/36 | __/16 |
| | __/16 | __/36 | __/16 |
| | __/16 | __/36 | __/16 |
| | __/16 | __/36 | __/16 |
| | __/16 | __/36 | __/16 |
| | __/16 | __/36 | __/16 |
| | __/16 | __/36 | __/16 |
| | __/16 | __/36 | __/16 |
| | __/16 | __/36 | __/16 |
| | __/16 | __/36 | __/16 |
| | __/16 | __/36 | __/16 |
| | __/16 | __/36 | __/16 |
| | __/16 | __/36 | __/16 |
| | __/16 | __/36 | __/16 |
| | __/16 | __/36 | __/16 |
| | __/16 | __/36 | __/16 |
| | __/16 | __/36 | __/16 |
| | __/16 | __/36 | __/16 |
| | __/16 | __/36 | __/16 |
| | __/16 | __/36 | __/16 |
| | __/16 | __/36 | __/16 |

Scoring: The higher the number, the stronger the learner is for that dimension. The score will show the learner's strength (higher numbers) or need (lower numbers).

*Scoring

12–16   Learners have a strong sense that they think they can succeed.

8–11   Learners have some sense that they can succeed.

4–7   Learners have a limited sense that they can succeed.

**Scoring

27–36   Learners have many reasons for wanting to succeed.

18–26   Learners have some reasons for wanting to succeed.

9–17   Learners have limited reasons for wanting to succeed.

## Assessing Schoolwide Configurations

If you are a teacher, use the Beyond Learners Survey (Teacher Assessment) on pages 44–45 to rate yourself; the texts, materials, and assessments you use; and schoolwide configurations. Tally each column and compute an overall score for each element. A score greater than 20 may suggest a stronger area, and a score of 20 or less may suggest an area in need of improvement. If you are a teacher-leader or administrator, use the Beyond Learners Survey (Faculty and Staff Assessment) on page 46. Average teachers' scores from the teacher surveys to identify schoolwide trends and needs. Use the findings of either survey to enhance joyful teaching in individual classrooms or schoolwide.

| Beyond Learners Survey (Teacher Assessment) | | | | | |
|---|---|---|---|---|---|
| Name: | | Date: | | | |
| **Factors** | **Statements** | **Rating Scale** | | | |
| Teacher | I know how to help… | | | | |
| | improve my learners' identities | | 1 | 2 | 3 |
| | improve my learners' confidence in their general abilities | | 1 | 2 | 3 |
| | improve my learners' confidence in their abilities to complete specific tasks | | 1 | 2 | 3 |
| | increase my learners' expectations for success | | 1 | 2 | 3 |
| | my learners want to succeed | | 1 | 2 | 3 |
| | my learners value learning | | 1 | 2 | 3 |
| | my students develop an internal locus of control | | 1 | 2 | 3 |
| | my students develop internalized reasons to stay engaged in tasks | | 1 | 2 | 3 |
| | my students develop self-regulating behaviors | | 1 | 2 | 3 |
| | my students develop positive social behavior | | 1 | 2 | 3 |
| | TOTALS | | | | |
| | OVERALL SCORE (total all 3 columns) | | | | |
| Texts and materials | The texts and materials I use help… | | | | |
| | improve my learners' identities | | 1 | 2 | 3 |
| | improve my learners' confidence in their general abilities | | 1 | 2 | 3 |
| | improve my learners' confidence in their abilities to complete specific tasks | | 1 | 2 | 3 |
| | increase my learners' expectations for success | | 1 | 2 | 3 |
| | my learners want to succeed | | 1 | 2 | 3 |
| | my learners value learning | | 1 | 2 | 3 |
| | my students develop an internal locus of control | | 1 | 2 | 3 |
| | my students develop internalized reasons to stay engaged in tasks | | 1 | 2 | 3 |
| | my students develop self-regulating behaviors | | 1 | 2 | 3 |
| | my students develop positive social behavior | | 1 | 2 | 3 |
| | TOTALS | | | | |
| | OVERALL SCORE (total all 3 columns) | | | | |

| Beyond Learners Survey (Teacher Assessment) (continued) | | | | |
|---|---|---|---|---|
| **Factors** | **Statements** | **Rating Scale** | | |
| Assessments | The assessments I select and use enable me to… | | | |
| | improve my learners' identities | 1 | 2 | 3 |
| | improve my learners' confidence in their general abilities | 1 | 2 | 3 |
| | improve my learners' confidence in their abilities to complete specific tasks | 1 | 2 | 3 |
| | improve my learners' expectations for success | 1 | 2 | 3 |
| | help my learners want to succeed | 1 | 2 | 3 |
| | help my learners value learning | 1 | 2 | 3 |
| | help my students develop an internal locus of control | 1 | 2 | 3 |
| | help my students develop internalized reasons to stay engaged in tasks | 1 | 2 | 3 |
| | help my students develop self-regulating behaviors | 1 | 2 | 3 |
| | help my students develop positive social behavior | 1 | 2 | 3 |
| | TOTALS | | | |
| | OVERALL SCORE (total all 3 columns) | | | |
| Schoolwide configurations | Our school focuses on factors that… | | | |
| | positively affect learners' identities | 1 | 2 | 3 |
| | increase learners' confidence in their general abilities | 1 | 2 | 3 |
| | increase learners' confidence in their abilities to complete specific tasks | 1 | 2 | 3 |
| | raise learners' expectations for success | 1 | 2 | 3 |
| | increase learners' desire to succeed | 1 | 2 | 3 |
| | help students value learning | 1 | 2 | 3 |
| | help improve students' internal locus of control | 1 | 2 | 3 |
| | help students develop internalized reasons to stay engaged in tasks | 1 | 2 | 3 |
| | encourage students to develop self-regulating behaviors | 1 | 2 | 3 |
| | improve students' use of positive social behaviors | 1 | 2 | 3 |
| | TOTALS | | | |
| | OVERALL SCORE (total all 3 columns) | | | |

| Beyond Learners Survey (Faculty and Staff Assessment) | | | | |
|---|---|---|---|---|
| Teacher/Staff | Total scores for each element (from Beyond Learners Survey–Teacher Assessment) | | | |
| | Teacher | Texts & materials | Assessments | Schoolwide configurations |
| | | | | |
| | | | | |
| | | | | |
| | | | | |
| | | | | |
| | | | | |
| | | | | |
| | | | | |
| | | | | |
| | | | | |
| | | | | |
| | | | | |
| | | | | |
| | | | | |
| | | | | |
| | | | | |
| | | | | |
| | | | | |
| | | | | |
| | | | | |
| | | | | |
| | | | | |
| | | | | |
| | | | | |
| Average score | | | | |
| Does this meet the standard? (20+) | | | | |

# CHAPTER 3

# Implementing Joyful Learning

After completing Affective Dimension Profiles of their students, Mike, Mary, and Kathy meet again. Kathy says, "I feel like I know my students and myself much better after using the profiles. Now I'm wondering how I can make sense of all of this information to improve my instruction."

Mary and Mike confess they feel the same way. Mike suggests they need a plan "to help us figure it out. Maybe we should start by looking at our own instruction in the whole group, small groups, and with individual students to see if the teaching strategies we use support joyful learning."

"That might be a good starting place, but wouldn't we also need to pay attention to what we learned about school community and environment?" Mary asks. "If we have a comprehensive plan, it might help remind us why we are doing what we are doing."

"I like that," says Kathy. "And when we come up with new ideas, we can see how they fit in the overall plan."

As Mary, Mike, and Kathy have realized, data-driven instruction is at the heart of joyful learning. Even with a joyful learning mindset, to improve instruction teachers still need to be able to make sense of the data they collect. They also need to be able to choose teaching strategies that will help them move from evaluation to implementation. Selecting the "right" teaching strategy (or strategies) to use in any given lesson can seem daunting. Developing a plan that classifies teaching strategies into meaningful categories allows them to be easily accessed and used in more intentional, deliberate, and joyful ways.

In this chapter, we will show you how to implement such a comprehensive plan; we also identify some activities that can help you create a joyful learning environment. Joyful learning is built on awareness of the five motivational generalizations we discussed in Chapter 1 (adaptive self-efficacy and competence beliefs, adaptive attributions and beliefs about control, higher levels of interest and intrinsic motivation, higher levels of value, and goals). It also requires having created the assessment profiles presented in Chapter 2 and addressing the five elements that contribute to learners' identities (learners, teachers, texts and materials, assessments, and schoolwide configurations).

The third part of our joyful learning framework incorporates efforts in five learning environments and configurations: the school community, the physical (classroom) environment, whole-group instruction, small-group instruction, and individual instruction. In this chapter, we explore these environments and configurations, provide a rationale for addressing each one, present a structure to guide planning and implementing improvements, and offer sample instructional activities that exploit the advantages of each environment and configuration (see Figure 3.1).

### FIGURE 3.1
### Coordinating Learning Environments with Supportive Activities

| Learning Environment | Rationale | Structure | Activity |
|---|---|---|---|
| School community | Create a positive climate | Schoolwide projects | Make a Difference Day |
| Physical environment | Have students connect learning and identity | Identity builders | Artifact displays |
| Whole-group instruction | Engage all learners | Active participation and thinking | Six Boxes |
| Small-group instruction | Provide social interaction | Group projects | Connected text sets |
| Individual instruction | Provide choice and incorporate interests | Focused workshops | Heroes |

Many instructional structures, strategies, and activities can contribute to joyful learning. Our intent here is to give you a starting point to build on as you continue to develop a joyful learning environment. When selecting activities to enhance a comprehensive joyful learning plan, bear in mind that they should

- Transcend content areas and grade levels;
- Enable teachers to use readily available resources;
- Fit into existing schoolwide and classroom routines;
- Propel learners toward thinking, wanting, and knowing how to succeed; and
- Lead to both affective (joyful) and cognitive (learning) outcomes.

## School Community

The purpose of focusing on the schoolwide community is to create a positive climate for joyful learning. The goal is to create a safe environment that supports the growth of the whole child and incorporates the supports and scaffolds needed to make this happen (ASCD, 2007). A sense of school community can be promoted by something as simple as a mascot that helps students identify who they are and engenders a sense of belonging. Schoolwide routines—ranging from how students are expected to treat one another to how the school handles morning announcements—also can create a positive learning climate and sense of belonging.

Focusing on the schoolwide community can help students understand that their school represents how communities outside schools work and how all in the community can work for the common good of the whole. As Martin Maehr has noted,

> Societies can hardly exist and properly function unless members largely respond to the needs of the community as a whole—"paying their dues," and contributing their time, talent and knowledge to the well-being not only of their immediate family but also the wider society—indeed to all that have need of their help. (2012, p. 12)

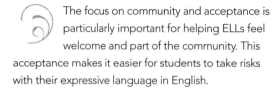 The focus on community and acceptance is particularly important for helping ELLs feel welcome and part of the community. This acceptance makes it easier for students to take risks with their expressive language in English.

In other words, students need to understand that "mi" is only one note of the music scale and that the right combination of notes is needed in order to make pleasant music, as are many different musicians all coordinated by a knowledgeable conductor.

## The Structure: Schoolwide Projects

As with effective and purposeful teaching, planning for what should occur in the schoolwide context and implementing that plan bolsters the structure. There are various ways to plan and implement such a structure (see, e.g., Schlechty, 2011); drawing from both research and our collective teaching experiences, we suggest following five steps:

1. Brainstorm and establish what you want to accomplish.
2. Decide individual responsibilities and a leader for the project.
3. Establish a goal and create and use a timeline to monitor progress.
4. Take action.
5. Come together as a community to celebrate successes.

**Activity: Make a Difference Day.** Created by the staff of *USA Weekend Magazine* in 1992, the purpose of Make a Difference Day is to do something for others in your community on the fourth Saturday in October. It is an excellent vehicle for creating a sense of community because students, teachers, and administrators collectively identify and agree on a project, and work to complete it.

Participating in a community activity helps students develop civic responsibility, build self-esteem, learn how to work together, appreciate diversity, and build cognitive (academic) skills (Make a Difference Day, n.d.). Schools benefit by increasing student motivation, extending learning beyond the classroom, and strengthening the relationship between school and community. Make a Difference Day also expands students' idea of "community" beyond their school and their region, by participating in a nationwide event. The Make a Difference Day website (http://www.usaweekend.com/article/ 99999999/MDDAY/90917001) has general and weekly planning guides for teachers that include project ideas and curriculum connections.

## Physical (Classroom) Environment

Identifying themselves as learners who can succeed is essential for students to grow. One way to focus on building their identities as learners is to create a physical classroom environment that shows your students as learners.

In one school, students have a plastic sleeve attached to their lockers. They use the sleeve to display an artifact that shows something about their learning. One student's sleeve holds a graph showing the texts he has read; another student's sleeve shows a picture of what she created in science.

Displays of student learning are sure ways to build a classroom environment that conveys positive learning identities. Being able to showcase individual learning and accomplishments, as well as viewing the learning and accomplishments of other students, conveys to students that they are an essential part of the classroom community and helps them build an identity as learners.

### The Structure: Identity Builders

Identity-building projects require students to actively interact with their learning and make links between what they learn and themselves, their knowledge, and their own experiences. When designing an identity-building project, it's important to take the following actions:

1. Decide what it is you want students to identify with (e.g., learning in general, scientists, mathematicians, social science experts, competent language users).

2. Arrange your classroom so that it includes a display area, wall, or other means of exhibiting the projects or artifacts (this might even include a screen on which images or PowerPoint presentations are projected) that represent students as learners.

3. Incorporate time in the school day for students to look at, interact with, and discuss the displays.

4. Incorporate time every day for students to add to their projects; allow them to discuss and explain what the new addition or improvement represents about themselves.

A great identity-building option for ELLs is to celebrate their bilingualism. This can be incorporated in any classroom display by incorporating captions in students' native languages (which highlights the fact that these students are learning in two or more languages) or otherwise highlighting students' (hidden) strengths.

**The Activity: Artifact Displays.** Kim is a 4th grade teacher who consciously tries to help her students see themselves as learners with many different identities, and to help them understand and identify with other capable, like-minded learners. She takes pictures of her students as they are completing various activities, and then has them choose the ones that they think show engaged learners. Her students write captions for their pictures and display them on a wall labeled "Identifying with Learning and Learners." Her students regularly go on "gallery walks" to reinforce their own identities as learners and help them see their classmates as learners, too.

## Whole-Group Instruction

Keeping all students engaged in joyful learning as they learn to appreciate content makes learning more likely. One way to accomplish engagement is to heed the advice of Jere Brophy (2008), who contended that there are ways teachers can design instruction that will help students both value and appreciate the content of that instruction. These include identifying and teaching content that applies to students' everyday lives, showing students how that content plays out in their everyday experiences, and scaffolding their learning. It also helps ensure that teachers focus on the context as much as the learners as a part of the learning process. Context influences one's ability to perform, hence learn; as Maehr (2012) noted, "While from time to time blame for apparent disinterest in classroom learning activities is placed on the child, likely more often it is the case that disinterest is largely a product of the original learning context" (p. 12).

Another way to keep students engaged is to use what Durrell (1956) called *every pupil response* techniques, which is similar to Himmele and Himmele's (2011) *total participation techniques*. The idea is to actively engage all students in a whole-class lesson by providing them with multiple ways to respond to posed questions or scenarios. In Himmele and Himmele's words, these strategies "allow for all students to demonstrate, at the same time, active participation and cognitive engagement in the topic being studied" (p. 7).

## The Structure: Active Participation and Thinking

The basis for the structure for whole-group instruction is the belief that all students can participate. Starting from this position, brainstorm and consider available options you have to encourage all students to participate. Himmele and Himmele (2011) suggested that students use individual dry-erase pens and boards, response cards, yes/no cards, and decks of number cards. We have also used multiple-choice wheels and laminated hands (purchased at dollar stores). Newer technology such as clicker response systems offers another option for responding and gives the advantage of being able to store data and track classroom trends for effective whole-group instruction,

1. Frame your requests for response around high-cognition activities. Himmele and Himmele stressed that participation techniques can be used to promote engagement with many learning outcomes; combining high participation with high cognition offers additional learning advantages.

2. Choose the response technique that best fits the learning outcome. As Himmele and Himmele explained, all types of learning can be evidenced with all-group responses.

**Activity: Six Boxes.** Six boxes is an activity we have used to frontload reading lessons, although it can be adapted easily for use in any content area. This activity supports students' convergent thinking, establishing personal connections, making and revising predictions, and self-assessing.

When setting up whole-group instruction, it is important to consider students' language proficiency levels. Students in early stages of mastering English may experience a "silent period," during which they may not be ready to produce verbal responses. Providing vocabulary scaffolding, building background, and encouraging choral responses are ideal for these learners. The activity we discuss here includes front-loading, vocabulary building, comprehensible input, and meaningful interactions to enhance the comprehension and participation of ELLs.

In each of six boxes on a sheet of paper, students respond to a prompt that links information from the text to themselves, their knowledge, and their own experience (see Figure 3.2). Here's the basic process for six boxes:

1. Give students five to eight words from a text that the group or class is getting ready to read. After a few minutes of review, ask stu-

---

**FIGURE 3.2**
**Active Participation and Thinking: Six Boxes Teaching Strategy**

| 1 | 2 | 3 |
|---|---|---|
| *Activity:* Students write a list of words that are similar to sample vocabulary from the text or relate to the identified theme. | *Activity:* Students write about a memory or experience that relates to theme or topic. | *Activity:* After reviewing the cover or sample illustration and revisiting the vocabulary and possible theme, students write their predictions about the text and state what elements they used in developing their predictions. |
| *Outcome:* Encourages convergent thinking | *Outcome:* Enables personal connections | *Outcome:* Encourages making predictions |

| 4 | 5 | 6 |
|---|---|---|
| *Activity:* Students revise their predictions based on additional vocabulary from the text. | *Activity:* After reading or hearing a selected portion of the text, students rate themselves on how well they predicted the topic or theme. | *Activity:* Students rate themselves on their participation in the overall activity. |
| *Outcome:* Enables revising predictions based on new information | *Outcome:* Enables confirming of predictions | *Outcome:* Enables student self-evaluation |

dents to discuss what they think the story or piece is going to be about. We often will pair students to develop and share predictions and explain their reasoning. Then, in Box 1, students record additional words that they have come up with that are related to the words originally provided. After working in groups to classify their words into two or three categories, students share and compare results as a class. This step bolsters learners' convergent thinking, helping them develop decision-making skills by collectively identifying themes and making vocabulary connections.

2. In Box 2, students write about a memory or personal experience that relates to the identified theme or subject and share this with a partner. This step helps students make a personal connection to the text, engaging them in the learning process.

3. Show students the cover of the book or a sample illustration; review the "evidence" so far (vocabulary, personal connection, visual). In Box 3, students write a prediction about the topic or theme of the text. Sharing their predictions with one another and explaining the basis for their prediction maintains engagement, develops process skills, and helps learners make connections between prior knowledge and the text.

4. Provide students with additional vocabulary from the text, including components such as character names, setting, and plot points. Add these words to a master vocabulary list that includes both the original words from the text and students' suggestions from Box 1. Review and discuss as a class, pointing out any "new" information that might bolster or change students' predictions. In Box 4, students write a revised or expanded prediction; sharing and discussing their predictions helps build their process skills in revising understanding based on new information.

5. After reading or listening to a selection from the text, students rate themselves (in Box 5) on a scale of 1 to 5 on how well their prediction matches the text. Giving themselves an overall participation score in Box 6 provides a culminating self-assessment activity that can increase student engagement across content areas and strengthen their identities as learners. It also provides feedback for teachers on areas of need across students in the classroom.

## Small-Group Instruction

Small-group instruction allows teachers to capitalize on social interactions that lead to joyful learning. In small groups, students have an opportunity to talk with one another and to participate in every aspect of an activity. In small groups, each participant is held accountable for completing tasks that reflect the group as a whole. This empowers students because each has information that the rest of the group needs; students in the small-group setting are dependent on one another.

### The Structure: Group Projects

Group projects are one way to take advantage of the joyful learning potential of small-group instruction; they also provide teachers the opportunity to support students in making connections and following themes or ideas across content areas and, potentially, throughout the school day. For this type of small-group instruction to be effective, try these steps:

1. Link group projects to a whole-class activity.

2. Vary your approach to grouping students. In some cases it may be helpful to group students and assign them specific resources or topics to explore. For other projects, display or distribute resources and allow learners to browse through them, selecting topics or materials they like, and then group students based on similar interest.

3. Plan how students will interact with the content within their small groups. You may need to establish roles or provide guidance to support students in assigning project responsibilities.

4. Establish a schedule for meeting with each group. Meeting with the group will enable you to monitor the progress and to ensure all students are participating and working together; you may need to model interpersonal skills such as inviting feedback from others or making compromises.

5. Plan a culminating activity for the class as a group. The activity might be a whole-day event where students share their projects; teach each other about their topics; or present, discuss, compare, and display projects or results.

**The Activity: Connected Text Sets.** We define *text sets* as collections of books, other print materials, and multimedia related to a common theme or topic. What makes the text sets "connected" is that different groups use different texts or selections from the same theme. Offering a variety of texts for different groups provides an opportunity for the class as a whole to make both connections and comparisons: students can discuss how their materials are alike and different, and how what they are learning from their selected texts relates to the overall theme and class knowledge about the subject. Choosing different reading levels and types of materials (magazine articles, online research briefs, and novels, for example) also allows for differentiation.

Darrell, a 2nd grade teacher, used connected text sets to help his students understand and apply the concept of making predictions (a reading comprehension strategy), learn about their pulse rates and discover how physical activity increases it, and learn more about physical activity. For reference, he turned to "Catch the Beat!" (Opitz & Davis-Duerr, 2010), a lesson plan developed for this purpose.

Darrell introduced the focus of the small-group activity by initiating a class discussion about how the strategy of making predictions (which they were using before and during reading) could be applied to different subjects. As an example, he asked them to "predict" the definition of *heart rate*. After students took their pulses, Darrell told them that this was called a *resting heart rate*. Next, the students predicted whether they thought the rate would increase, stay the same, or decrease if they marched around the room for three minutes. The students conducted this experiment and compared their postmarch heart rates to their resting heart rates. Darrell explained that "when you move, your heart rate goes up. When you move, you make your heart work harder. It has to push blood in and out more quickly than when you are sitting still. So if you want to have a strong heart, you have to move.

> Allow ELLs to browse through texts and select one they would like that builds background knowledge (as they view the images in the text) and matches their language and literacy skills. Facilitating discussion in small groups will reduce the anxiety of whole-group sharing and encourage students to take risks with their English.

You have to be physically active. And that is what you are going to be reading about today during small group reading time."

During small-group reading sessions that day, each group selected a different book from a text set that included *Run and Hike, Play and Bike: What is Physical Activity?* (Cleary, 2011); *Get Up and Go!* (Carlson, 2006); *Exercise and Play* (Senker, 2008); *We Like to Move: Exercise is Fun* (April, 2011); *Ready, Set, Skip!* (O'Connor, 2009); and *The Busy Body Book: A Kid's Guide to Fitness* (Rockwell, 2004). During their reading groups, the students made a list of physical activities.

Later, the class as a whole created a master list called, "Physical Activities We Can Do" and reviewed what they had learned about being physically active. Darrell extended student learning beyond the classroom by having students maintain an exercise log tracking their physical activities inside and outside school for a week. A connected text-set lesson on this topic could be extended for older students, by graphing student results, sharing information with other classrooms, or undertaking a whole-school physical fitness project.

## Individual Instruction

Individual instruction is perhaps one of the best ways to address and encourage student interest and choice. Individual instruction allows students to choose and explore topics of interest and teachers a variety of ways to encourage and implement independent student learning. For example, Guccione (2011a) used "Afternoon Inquiry" in her 2nd grade classroom to further student learning about a variety of topics, and described how she set up the experience so that she was comfortable implementing such an open-ended activity. From *Joyful Reading Resource Kit*, Reis (2009) addressed individual instruction and included directions and forms for teachers and students to use. Both of these are fitting examples of how to use individual instruction based on student interest and choice; regardless of the structure, the important thing to remember is that independent student work is focused on something that individual students want to discover or explore.

## The Structure: Focused Workshop

Woodworkers, artists, writers, scientists, engineers, and mathematicians all have "workshops" where they can delve into their craft for extended periods of time. Building on the work of educators such as Atwell (1987), Graves (1983), Calkins (1990), and Fletcher & Portalupie (2001), our "focused workshop" has many of the same characteristics.

A focused workshop starts with a whole-class, teacher-directed focus lesson intended to guide students as they independently use resources and materials to learn. Lessons should evolve from what learners know and what they are showing they need to know, as defined by local standards and revealed through student assessment. Because a focused workshop attempts to build joyful learning by capitalizing on the dimensions of interest and choice, it is important to select a broad topic that will lend itself to multiple materials, processes for learning, and products from learning.

After the focus lesson, provide students with the time and resources to work independently on activities that relate to the lesson; hold all students to the same expectations regardless of perceived achievement levels, providing support as needed. Independent projects allow students to self-select materials and resources that suit both their interest and their level of knowledge or ability; allowing some flexibility in the nature of the resulting product also empowers students by letting them show what they know in a way that suits them. Ongoing response activities and individual conferences allow you to track progress and provide guidance and support as needed.

After the workshop session, bring students back together as a whole class to share their new knowledge. Extension activities will lead to conversations across and beyond students' learning experiences and also create a sense of community within the classroom. Figure 3.3 provides some tips for successfully implementing a focused workshop in your classroom.

Focused workshops provide a natural model of differentiation guided by student interest and choice. The motivation and engagement aspects of self-selected research and discovery positively impact the meaning making with complex texts among ELLs (Guccione, 2011b). This type of inquiry and workshop builds on ELLs' prior knowledge, curiosity, and experiences while scaffolding their language and literacy development.

| FIGURE 3.3 **Focused Workshop** | |
|---|---|
| Part 1: Focus lesson | As appropriate, incorporate personal examples in discussing the topic and encourage students to share their existing knowledge and experience. Model how to do the independent activity. Conducting a short whole-class sample activity will ensure all students understand the process. Have students offer additional examples and information from their individual resources as a whole-class activity. Set a clear purpose for continuing the learning, and provide visible/written directions and instructions for independent work. |
| Part 2: Independent work | Provide support as needed to individual students. Incorporate periods of whole-class discussion to reinforce and help guide individual student work. Hold individual conferences with students to provide additional guidance and support as needed. |
| Part 3: Culminating activity | Set up a community-sharing forum that systematically invites students to share how they completed the learning experience. Provide some time for students to have conversations about their learning experiences across the classroom community. Have students complete self-evaluations reflecting on something that they did well and something that they could improve on next time. Talk about these in the large-group setting. |

**Activity: Exploring Our Heroes.** The topic of heroes is appropriate to all grade levels and different content areas, and it provides an opportunity for students to explore the real-life examples of prosocial behaviors and essential noncognitive skills such as perseverance, ways to face adversity, and resilience. In planning a focused workshop on heroes, consider how you want to frame the focus lesson, which in turn will guide student exploration. Posing key questions that prompt students to think about and explore prosocial behaviors and noncognitive skills will provide ongoing teachable moments about these components of joyful learning. Key questions for whole-class discussion might include the following:

- What are some things a hero might do?
- Who is someone you know who you think is a hero and someone you admire?
- Who is a hero who faced something terrible and succeeded?

- Who is a hero who overcame a challenge?
- What are some personality traits of heroes?

During the class discussion, identify connections among student responses to help shape the key questions and activities that will guide students' explorations about heroes. Discussing key questions also can support your interaction with individual students, as they work on the products that will show what they have learned. Key questions should also shape the follow-up extension activities that will help unite the class as a community of learners and lead to conversations across and beyond this particular learning experience.

Once the focused workshop begins, use some time in each class session or day to teach a focus lesson that relates to the content or processes being learned by students. For example, an early lesson could be showing students how to stay focused as they explore multiple resources. Modeling the use of and encouraging students to use a graphic organizer can help them remain focused on the key questions and the aspects of their hero that most interest them (Education Place has a variety of different organizers for varying grade levels at www.eduplace.com/graphicorganizer/).

Throughout the focused workshop process, provide scaffolds through a gradual release of responsibility in which you move from *I* (modeling and demonstrating) to *we* (students working under your supervision) to *you* (students working independently). Make sure students have a clear purpose for the work they are doing during any class, and be systematic about meeting with and guiding or supporting learners as they work independently.

Always leave some time at the end of each class session or day for students to come back together as a community to share what and how they have been learning about their heroes. Periodically, provide students with a simple self-evaluation form that has them reflect on what they did well during the workshop time, what they learned or accomplished, what they might improve next time, and what else they want to explore.

Although extension and culminating activities will be based on themes identified by the students (and their age, grade level, and the content area), they might include a public gallery walk where learners display and share what they have learned; a class wiki, website, or webquest; student performances; PowerPoint presentations or videos; or a class newspaper or book. The effect of the focused workshop should not end when students complete the assignment. Continuing to discuss and reflect on their heroes (as models of prosocial behaviors and noncognitive skills) can have an effect beyond the classroom walls.

Now that you've learned about the power of joyful learning—what it is, why it is so beneficial, and how to use it in your classroom—you may still have questions. In Chapter 4, we'll try to anticipate your questions.

# Using Joyful Learning to Support Education Initiatives

At this point, you understand the concept of joyful learning—what it is, why it is important, and how to implement it schoolwide and within individual classrooms. However, you may still have some questions about how to stay focused on helping students to rediscover the joy of learning given the contemporary demands that you face. We anticipated some of your questions based on our work with teachers who strive to refine their teaching daily. As in our past work (Opitz & Ford, 2008), we frame these questions (as we hear so often) with "Yeah, but . . . ."

## How Can Joyful Learning Be Implemented Within RTI Frameworks?

The current reauthorization of the Individuals with Disabilities Education Act (passed by Congress in 2004) encouraged schools to catch learning problems as early as possible, thereby shrinking the number of students who might otherwise be referred to special education for additional services. Response to Intervention (RTI) is a research-based approach many schools use in carrying out this legislation.

In spite of the way it is sometimes interpreted, RTI is not a single, specific approach to teaching; like joyful learning, it is a process of implementing high-quality, scientifically researched instruction, monitoring student progress, and adjusting instruction based on student response. The goal of RTI is to expand the range and diversity of prevention and intervention options to enhance outcomes for all students. And what better way to do this than to focus on joyful learning?

Volumes have been and continue to be written about RTI. What is most pertinent to answering the question at hand are the guiding principles of RTI (International Reading Association Commission on Response to Intervention, 2009), which align with joyful learning (see Figure 4.1).

RTI is about designing and delivering the best possible instruction and paying attention to how children perform. The goal is to continuously discover what children know and need to know in order to help them progress—and that is exactly what joyful learning is all about. In some ways, joyful learning is an expanded view of RTI in that it focuses on learners' cognitive *and* noncognitive learning processes; it focuses on the whole child.

Unfortunately, many schools' RTI plans assess, address, and monitor student behavior (i.e., noncognitive learning) through systems completely separate from cognitive learning processes. Although some schools integrate positive behavioral intervention and support (PBIS) programs within RTI frameworks to address behavioral concerns, PBIS often is implemented separately from cognitive intervention programs. RTI implementation that doesn't focus on the whole child through an integrated system, and instead consists

| FIGURE 4.1 | |
|---|---|
| **RTI and Joyful Learning** | |
| **Guiding principle** | **Sample statement** |
| Instruction | Instruction needs to be of the highest quality and engage all students. |
| Responsive teaching and differentiation | Teacher-student interaction should guide selection of instructional techniques and materials. |
| Assessment | Assessment needs to be multidimensional. |
| Collaboration | All professionals work together to create the best learning climate for the entire school community. |
| Systematic and comprehensive approaches | A schoolwide model that encompasses a systematic approach to assessment and instruction is essential. |
| Expertise | Teacher expertise provides the basis for effective learning. |

of interventions that focus exclusively on behavioral or cognitive issues, will fall short of its goals. We believe that if learners don't perceive that they can be successful, value the outcomes, or feel safe in their environment, any cognitive intervention will not achieve its desired result—no matter how beneficial it may be or how well it is delivered (*fidelity*).

So, how can you integrate the essential components of joyful learning within an RTI framework? One practical idea is to think carefully about what we know about self-evaluation. *Self-evaluation* involves learners in self-judgment, often leading them to awareness of their control over their progress and performance. This process can build self-confidence, providing motivation for setting new goals and making new efforts—which in turn often are linked to improved performance. In fact, according to Hattie (2012), student predictions of their score or grade on a test to be taken and their expectations to succeed at this level are highly accurate.

Monitoring progress is a critical aspect of most RTI frameworks, so why not involve learners in that monitoring, as informants on their own learning? Learners can assist with collecting data on their own learning and charting these data over time. Student-driven data collection offers many opportunities to engage learners in conversations about why they are improving and to identify and set goals. In the end, when learners know that they can control their behaviors (whether cognitive, noncognitive, or both), that knowledge strengthens their identity, raises their expectations for success, and provides more possibilities for joyful learning.

## How Does Joyful Learning Address Achievement Gaps?

The real question: Can joyful learning help accelerate the growth of all learners? Focusing on joyful learning as we define and explain it in this book enables teachers to give more attention to an essential dimension of differentiation: acceleration. Rather than doing different things for different learners, *acceleration* implies targeting specific factors for specific learners that will cause them to make greater gains. Addressing both cognitive and noncognitive needs leads to joyful learning. Consciously using different grouping techniques, assigning independent learning projects, and introducing students to a wide variety of texts and materials all help motivate and engage students, which pays off with greater cognitive and noncognitive gains for students. At a minimum, students will be less resistant to the learning opportunities they need the most. Acceleration and joyful learning go hand in hand, particularly if we bear in mind some essential guidelines:

- **Keep overall goals in mind throughout the day.** If we are going to help all students be successful, that goal needs to be present in our minds throughout the school day, throughout the school week, and throughout the school year.
- **Design whole-group lessons for all learners.** Because targeting instruction is more effectively achieved in small groups or individually, we need to consider whether the time devoted to whole-class instruction is appropriate and whether it is engaging for all learners.
- **Ensure that small-group instruction effectively targets instructional needs.** In small groups, the focus should be on teaching learners (as opposed to teaching materials, texts, and programs). This focus necessitates focusing on and strengthening our ability to coach learners as they work in small groups.
- **Ensure that independent work is powerful work.** We need to tighten up existing individualized approaches so that all learners are supported in their choice of appropriate materials and focused on high expectations before, during, and after the independent work.

## How Does Joyful Learning Correlate to Standards?

School reform movements are ubiquitous and will continue to affect and influence the classroom environment. In the field of education, we are constantly searching for newer and better ways to educate our youth, and this search is most often fueled by findings from researchers in many different disciplines. Currently, the Common Core State Standards are in the media spotlight, and joyful learning can be part of any school's implementation of the standards.

Consider the emphasis on *rigor*. The standards stress the need to "pursue with equal intensity [students'] conceptual understanding, procedural skill and fluency, and applications" (National Governors Association

Center for Best Practices, Council of Chief State School Officers [NGACBP/ CCSSO], 2012, p. 3). When students are experiencing joyful learning, they are pursuing learning that requires rigor. In addition, the standards note that scaffolding to support learners as needed to help them succeed with more complex tasks is as important as rigor (see, e.g., NGACBP/CCSSO, 2010a, 2010b). Models of how to address multiple standards have led to visions of instruction that uses integrated themes. This type of instruction allows for greater learner involvement by having students conduct self-selected inquiries using a variety of materials at multiple levels in social contexts (see, e.g., the Common Core Curriculum Maps, www.commoncore.org/maps/). Because the standards call on teachers to use real content and scaffolded instruction that allows for challenge, choice, interest, and social interaction, they reflect many of the components that we have discussed as being at the heart of joyful learning.

Websites such as Expeditionary Learning (http://elschools.org/) provide support and resources to educators who want to implement standards yet stay focused on student creativity. Teachers can engage students with projects that capture their interest and lead them not only to accomplish several standards but to experience joyful learning. Most of these successful projects cross disciplines and capitalize on using the arts to showcase learning. For example, the Expeditionary Learning project "Wisconsin for Kids by Kids" (see http://elschools.org/our-results/gallery/wisconsin-kids-kids) culminated in a book created by middle school students; the result of their research not only provided a social studies resource for other students throughout the state but also raised funds for a reading program at the school.

## How Does Joyful Learning Support the Focus on Accountability and Assessment?

As we discussed earlier in this book, engagement usually occurs when three key conditions are present:

• Learners feel that the task in front of them is within their reach (*self-efficacy*).

- Learners value the outcome from the task.
- The task is completed in an environment in which learners feel safe.

If any one of these conditions is not present, levels of engagement drop. If your students have the ability to be successful with state-mandated exams, make sure you remind them verbally and through preparation activities that these are tasks at which they can succeed. If you believe you are creating a safe atmosphere in which to take the tests, then address more directly the stress, anxiety, and pressure students may bring to these situations. Addressing the pressures may be especially important if negative consequences (summer school, retention, low grades, retraction of special privileges) are the primary vehicle for motivation. More times than not, the difficulty with engagement related to state-mandated tests is that students have little reason to value the outcome. Unlike self-selected standardized assessments where scholarships, college admission, college credit, or professional licensure might be at stake, these externally mandated tests provide few benefits to increase individual commitment.

Unfortunately, researchers have spent little time exploring how to get students to value tasks such as these. As new assessment consortia embrace more performance-based assessments that actively involve learners in tasks that allow some choice, and encourage students to work with others on topics of greater interest in showing what they know, perhaps levels of engagement will increase.

Listening to what students have to say and heeding their advice also might prove helpful for engaging them. In talking with students, Cushman (2010) found three prevalent ideas among them:

- *Students want to be assessed all the time, and not just with high-stakes tests.* Students commented that the teachers they felt helped them learn the most were those who served as coaches, watching for what they could do well and what they needed to improve in order to best understand given content.

- *Students want their progress, large and small, to be charted.* They want their teachers to track their growth and to celebrate their ongoing progress.

• *Students want teachers to use performances as a way to assess their understanding.* They value showing others what they learned by performing in some way. Speaking in favor of performances to assess, a student named Rubin commented, "With a test or writing a paper, people won't be so interested. If you pass it, then, okay, you're going to get a grade. It's not like you really need to push yourself to go beyond what's going to be on the test" (p. 110).

One advantage of the new assessments emerging from groups such as the Partnership for Assessment of Readiness for College and Careers (PARCC; see www.parcconline.org) and the Smarter Balanced Assessment Consortium (Smarter Balanced; www.smarterbalanced.org/about/) is that these may be more compatible with joyful learning. Our suggestion is to look at samples of assessments and analyze the learning processes required by test items. For example, a 6th grade practice item from Smarter Balanced engages learners in preparing an argumentative article about advocating for or against the use of school and community gardens (Smarter Balanced, n.d.). This would fit with our suggestion of engaging students in schoolwide projects, the school community being a key area in which to promote joyful learning. The processes used to make decisions about real schoolwide projects (i.e., read and view information, take and organize arguments for and against, prepare position statements, present those arguments) will prepare learners to handle similar simulated tasks on the new assessments.

An educator shared how the students in her environmental charter school were reading proposed legislation to change open mining laws in an environmentally sensitive area of the state. They were reading, viewing, and listening to information from multiple sources. They were taking notes and organizing thoughts as they prepared position papers to send to their local legislators. Ongoing learning experiences like these prepare students to handle similar problem-solving and organizational tasks on the new exams.

The four questions in this chapter are conversation starters about joyful learning. We hope that you, like Mike, Kathy, and Mary, will continue the conversation as you explore insights and ideas for how to bring about joyful learning in your classrooms and schools.

# References

Allington, R. & Johnston, P. (Eds.). (2002). *Reading to learn: Lessons from exemplary fourth-grade classrooms.* New York: Guilford.

Ames, C. (1992). Classrooms: Goals, structures, and student motivation. *Journal of Educational Psychology, 84,* 261–271. http://dx.doi.org/10.1037/0022-0663.84.3.261

April, E. (2011). *We like to move: Exercise is fun.* Chino Valley, AZ: Hohm Press.

ASCD. (2007). *The learning compact redefined: A call to action. A report of the Commission on the Whole Child.* Alexandria, VA: Author.

Atwell, N. (1987). *In the middle.* Portsmouth, NH: Heinemann.

Bandura, A. (1997). *Self-efficacy: The exercise of control.* New York: Freeman.

Britten, T., & Lyle, G. (1984). What's love got to do with it? [Recorded by Tina Turner]. On *Private dancer* [Record]. Los Angeles, CA: Capitol Records.

Brophy, J. (2008). Developing students' appreciation for what is taught in school. *Educational Psychologist, 43,* 132–141. http://dx.doi.org/10.1080/00461520701756511

Calkins, L. (1990). *The art of teaching writing.* Portsmouth, NH: Heinemann.

Cambourne, B. (1995). Towards an educationally relevant theory of literacy learning: Twenty years of inquiry. *The Reading Teacher, 49,* 182–202.

Cambourne, B. (2001). Conditions for literacy learning: Why do some students fail to learn to read? Ockham's razor and the conditions of learning. *The Reading Teacher, 54,* 784–786.

Carlson, N. (2006). *Get up and go!* New York: Puffin Books.

Castelli, D. M., Hillman, C. H., Buck, S. M., & Erwin, H. E. (2007). Physical fitness and academic achievement in third- and fifth-grade students. *Journal of Sport & Exercise Psychology, 29,* 239–252.

Centers for Disease Control and Prevention. (2010, July). *The association between school-based physical activity, including physical education, and academic performance.* Atlanta, GA: U.S. Department of Health and Human Services. Retrieved from http://www.cdc.gov/healthyyouth/health_and_academics/pdf/pa-pe_paper.pdf

Chinich, M. (Producer), & Hughes, J. (Director). (1986). *Ferris Bueller's day off* [Motion picture]. United States: Paramount.

Chugani, H. T. (1998). Biological basis of emotions: Brain systems and brain development. *Pediatrics, 102,* 1225–1229.

Cleary, B. P. (2011). *Run and hike, play and bike: What is physical activity?* Minneapolis, MN: Millbrook Press.

Cummins, J., & Sayers, D. (1995). *Brave new schools: Challenging cultural illiteracy through global learning networks.* New York: St. Martin's Press.

Cushman, K. (2010). *Fires in the mind: What kids can tell us about motivation and mastery.* San Francisco: Jossey-Bass.

Deci, E. L., & Ryan, R. M. (1985). *Intrinsic motivation and self-determination in human behavior.* New York: Basic.

Dolezal, S. E., Welsh, L. M., Pressley, M., & Vincent, M. M. (2003). How nine third-grade teachers motivate student academic engagement. *Elementary School Journal, 103,* 239–267. http://dx.doi.org/10.1086/499725

Durrell, D. (1956). *Improving reading instruction.* New York: World Book.

Dweck, C. (2009). *Mindset: The new psychology of success.* New York: Ballantine.

Echevarria, J., Short, D., & Vogt, M. E. (2011). *Making content comprehensible for English learners: The SIOP Model.* Boston: Pearson.

Farrington, C. A., Roderick, M., Allensworth, E., Nagaoka, J., Keyes, T. S., Johnson, D. W., & Beechum, N. O. (2012). *Teaching adolescents to become learners: The role of noncognitive factors in shaping school performance: A critical literature review.* Chicago: University of Chicago Consortium on Chicago School Research.

Fiedler, K. (2012). *Listening to the voices of boys: A mosaic approach to exploring the motivation to engage in reading.* Unpublished doctoral dissertation, University of Northern Colorado, Greeley.

Fletcher, R., & Portalupie. J. (2001). *Writing workshop: The essential guide.* Portsmouth, NH: Heinemann.

Fredericks, J. A., Blumenfeld, P. C., & Paris, A. H. (2004). School engagement: Potential of the concept, state of the evidence. *Review of Educational Research, 74,* 59–109. http://dx.doi.org/10.3102/00346543074001059

Gonzalez, V., Brusca-Vega, R., & Yawkey, T. (1997). *Assessment and instruction of culturally and linguistically diverse students.* Needham Heights, MA: Allyn & Bacon.

Graves, D. (1983). *Writing: Teachers and children at work.* Portsmouth, NH: Heinemann.

Grumet, M. (1999). Romantic research: Why we love to read. In S. Appel (Ed.), *Psychoanalysis and pedagogy* (pp. 147–165). Westport, CT: Bergin & Garvey.

Guccione, L. M. (2011a). In a world of mandates: Making space for inquiry. *The Reading Teacher, 64,* 515–519. http://dx.doi.org/10.1598/RT.64.7.5

Guccione, L. M. (2011b). Integrating literacy and inquiry for English learners. *The Reading Teacher, 64,* 567–577. http://dx.doi.org/10.1598/RT.64.8.2

Guthrie, J., & Wigfield, A. (1997). *Reading engagement: Motivating readers through integrated instruction.* Newark, DE: International Reading Association.

Guthrie, J. T. (2011). Best practices in motivating students to read. In L. Morrow, and L. Gambrell (Eds.), *Best practices in literacy instruction* (4th ed., pp. 177–198). New York: Guilford.

Hall, L. (2009). Struggling reader, struggling teacher: An examination of student-teacher transactions with reading instruction and text in social studies. *Research in the Teaching of English, 43,* 287–309.

Halliday, M. (1975). *Explorations in the functions of language.* London: Arnold.

Hattie, J. (2012). *Visible learning for teachers: Maximizing impact on learning.* New York: Routledge.

Himmele, P., & Himmele, W. (2011). *Total participation techniques: Making every student an active learner.* Alexandria, VA: ASCD.

International Reading Association Commission on Response to Intervention. (2009). *Response to Intervention: Guiding principles for educators from the International Reading Association.* Newark, DE: Author. Retrieved from www.reading.org/Libraries/resources/RTI_brochure_web.pdf

Jiménez, R. T. (1999). Literary lessons derived from the instruction of six Latina/Latino teachers. In B. M. Taylor, M. Graves, and P. Van den Broek (Eds.), *Reading for meaning: Fostering comprehension in the middle grades* (pp. 152–169), New York: Teachers College Press.

Johnston, P. (2004). *Choice words*. Portland, ME: Stenhouse.

Johnston, P. (2012). *Opening minds: Using language to change lives*. Portland, ME: Stenhouse.

Katz, L. G., & Chard, S. C. (2000). *Engaging children's minds: The project approach* (2nd ed.). Stamford, CT: Ablex.

Klingner, J. K., Artiles, A. J., Kozleski, E., Harry, B., Zion, S., Tate, W. . . . Riley, D. (2005). Addressing the disproportionate representation of culturally and linguistically diverse students in special education through culturally responsive educational systems. Retrieved from http://epaa.asu.edu/ojs/article/view/143.

Kohn, A. (1999). *Punished by rewards*. New York: Houghton Mifflin.

Krashen, S. D. (1987). *Principles and practice in second language acquisition*. Englewood Cliffs, NJ: Prentice Hall.

Layton, N. (2002). *The Sunday blues: A book for schoolchildren, schoolteachers, and anybody else who dreads Monday mornings*. Cambridge, MA: Candlewick Press.

Locke, E. A., & Latham, G. P. (2002). Building a practically useful theory of goal setting and task motivation: A 35-year odyssey. *American Psychologist, 57*, 705–717. http://dx.doi.org/10.1037/0003-066X.57.9.705

Maehr, M. L. (2012). *Encouraging a continuing personal investment in learning: Motivation as an instructional outcome*. Charlotte, NC: Information Age.

Make a Difference Day. (n.d.). *Why participate?* Retrieved from http://makeadifferenceday.com/getting-started/k-12-educators/

Medina, J. (2008). *Brain rules: 12 principles for surviving and thriving at work, home, and school*. Seattle, WA: Pear Press.

National Governors Association Center for Best Practices, Council of Chief State School Officers. (2010a). *Application of common core state standards for English language learners*. Washington, DC: Author. Retrieved from www.corestandards.org/assets/application-for-english-learners.pdf

National Governors Association Center for Best Practices, Council of Chief State School Officers. (2010b). *Common core state standards application to students with disabilities*. Washington, DC: Author. Retrieved from www.corestandards.org/assets/application-to-students-with-disabilities.pdf

National Governors Association Center for Best Practices, Council of Chief State School Officers. (2012, July). *K–8 publishers' criteria for the common core state standards for mathematics*. Retrieved from www.corestandards.org/assets/Math_Publishers_Criteria_K-8_Summer%20 2012_FINAL.pdf

O'Connor, J. (2009). *Ready, set, skip!* New York: Puffin Books.

Olson, K. (2009). *Wounded by school: Recapturing the joy in learning and standing up to old school culture*. New York: Teachers College Press.

Opitz, M., with Davis-Duerr, J. (2010). *Literacy lessons to help kids get fit and healthy*. New York: Scholastic.

Opitz, M. & Ford, M. (2008). *Do-able differentiation: Varying groups, texts, and supports to reach readers*. Portsmouth, N.H.: Heinemann.

Pawlak, R., Magarinos, A. M., Melchor, J., McEwen, B., & Strickland, S. (2003). Tissue plasminogen activator in the amygdala is critical for stress-induced anxiety-like behavior. *Nature Neuroscience, 6*, 168–174. http://dx.doi.org/10.1038/nn998

Pearson, P. D. (1996). Reclaiming the center. In M. Graves, P. van den Broek, & B. M. Taylor (Eds.), *The first R: Every child's right to read* (pp. 259–274). New York: Teachers College Press.

Pink, D. (2009). *Drive: The surprising truth about what motivates us.* New York: Riverhead.

Pintrich, P. R. (2003). A motivational science perspective on the role of student motivation in learning and teaching contexts. *Journal of Educational Psychology, 95,* 667–686. http://dx. doi.org/10.1037/0022-0663.95.4.667

Pressley, M. (2006). *Reading instruction that works: The case for balanced teaching.* New York: Guilford.

Pressley, M., Allington, R., Wharton-McDonald, R., Collins Block, C., & Mandel Morrow, L. (2001). *Learning to read: Lessons from exemplary first-grade classrooms.* New York: Guilford.

Rantala, T., & Maatta, K. (2012). Ten theses of the joy of learning at primary schools. *Early Child Development and Care, 182*(1), 87–105. http://dx.doi.org/10.1080/03004430.2010.545124

Ratey, J. J. (2008). *Spark: The revolutionary new science of exercise and the brain.* New York: Little, Brown.

Reis, S. M. (2009). *The joyful reading resource kit: Teaching tools, hands-on activities, and enrichment resources.* San Francisco: Jossey-Bass.

Rockwell, L. (2004). *The busy body book.* New York: Crown Books.

Rowan, B., Correnti, R., Miller, R., & Camburn, E. (2009). *School improvement by design: Lessons from a study of comprehensive school reform programs.* Retrieved from www.cpre.org

Rueda, R. (2011). *The 3 dimensions of improving student performance.* New York: Teachers College Press.

Schlechty, P. C. (2011). *Engaging students: The next level of working on the work.* San Francisco: Jossey-Bass.

Sell, C. (2007). *A cup of comfort for teachers: Heartwarming stories of people who mentor, motivate, and inspire.* Avon, MA: Adams Media.

Senker, C. (2008). *Exercise and play.* New York: Powerkids Press.

Shannon, P. (2012). *Reading wide awake: Politics, pedagogies, and possibilities.* New York: Teachers College Press.

Small, G. (2003). *Joyful learning: No one ever wants to go to recess!* Lanham, MD: Scarecrow Education.

Smarter Balanced Assessment Consortium. (n.d.) *SMARTER balanced assessment—Mathematics.* Retrieved from www.smarterbalanced.org/wordpress/wp-content/uploads/2012/09/ performance-tasks/garden.pdf

Stanton, K. (2007). *Papi's gift.* Honesdale, PA: Boyds Mills Press.

Tatum, A. (2009, June). *Literacy and African American boys: Shifting the paradigm.* Paper presented at the 28th University of Wisconsin Reading Research Symposium, Appleton, WI.

Tough, P. (2012). *How children succeed: Grit, curiosity, and the hidden power of character.* Boston: Houghton Mifflin.

Vogt, M., & Shearer, B. (2010). *Reading specialists and literacy coaches in the real world* (3rd ed.). New York: Pearson.

Waterman, A. S. (2005). When effort is enjoyed: Two studies of intrinsic motivation for personally salient activities. *Motivation and Emotion, 29,* 165–188. http://dx.doi.org/10.1007/ s11031-005-9440-4

Wigfield, A., & Eccles, J. (2002). *Development of achievement motivation.* San Diego, CA: Academic Press.

Willis, J. (2007). The neuroscience of joyful education. *Educational Leadership, 64* [Online]. Retrieved from www.ascd.org/publications/educational-leadership/summer07/vol64/num09/ The-Neuroscience-of-Joyful-Education.aspx

Wlodkowski, R. J., & Ginsberg, M. B. (1995). *Diversity and motivation: Culturally responsive teaching.* San Francisco: Jossey-Bass.

# Index

*Note:* JLF refers to Joyful Learning Framework and the letter *f* following a page number denotes a figure.

acceleration, 65–66
accountability
  JLF's support for, 67–69
  motivation and, 9
achievement gaps, 65–66
active participation and thinking
  in whole-group instruction,
  53–55, 54*f*
Affective Dimension Profile
  for classrooms, 42*f*
  function of, 37
  for students, 41*f*
  using the results of the, 40
affective engagement, 20
affective outcomes
  assessing and evaluating,
  33–34
  factors influencing, 30–31
Artifact Displays, 52
assessment/evaluation. *See also*
  specific elements; specific
  groups
  of affective outcomes, 33–34
  of engagement, 20–21,
  68–69
  JLF's support for, 67–69
  student advice on, 68–69
attainment form of value, 13*f*
attentive learners, 18

attributions, adaptive, 12*f*
autonomous pleasure, 14

behaviors, assessing, 20, 29*f*,
  41*f*
Beyond Learners Survey
  for faculty and staff, 46*f*
  for students, 37, 39*f*
  for teachers, 44–45*f*

challenge, assessing, 28*f*, 41*f*
classroom environment. *See*
  physical environment
committed learners, 18
competence beliefs
  instructional implication, 12*f*
  in the JLF framework, 11
competition, assessing, 29*f*, 41*f*
compliance, assessing, 28*f*, 41*f*
Connected Text Sets, 57–58
context
  focusing on, importance
  of, 52
  influence on the learner,
  22–23
control beliefs, instructional
  implication, 12*f*
cost form of value, 13*f*
curiosity, assessing, 27*f*, 41*f*

Disabilities Education Act, 63

educational priorities, JLF's
  support for
  accountability and
  assessment, support for,
  67–69
  achievement gaps,
  addressing, 65–66
  RTI frameworks, 63–65, 64*f*
  standards, correlation to,
  66–67
engagement
  assessing, 18, 20–21, 41*f*
  characteristics of, 18–19
  components of, 18, 26–27
  conditions necessary for,
  67–68
  defined, 17
  entertainment vs., 19
  joyful learning and, 17–21,
  22
  motivation and, 17–21
  outcomes for learners
  impacting, 25–30
  reasons for concern about,
  8–10
  strategies for, 18, 20, 52–53
  types of, 20

engagement *(cont'd)*
    whole-group instruction and,
        52–53
entertainment, 19–20
every pupil response techniques,
    52

focused workshops for individual
    instruction, 59–62, 60*f*
fun, building social relationships
    through, 20

goals
    instructional implication, 13*f*
    in the JLF framework, 11
group projects for small-group
    instruction, 56–58

high effort-liked activities, 19, 22

identity, assessing, 27*f*, 41*f*
identity building and the
    physical environment, 51–52
implementation. *See also* specific
    learning environments
    of JLF, reasons for, 21–23
    within RTI frameworks,
        63–65, 64*f*
importance, assessing, 28*f*, 41*f*
independent learning, 66
individual instruction
    activity: Exploring our
        Heroes, 60–62
    function of, 58
    in the JLF framework, 11
    the structure: focused
        workshop, 59–62, 60*f*
    supportive activities for, 48*f*
involvement, assessing, 28*f*, 41*f*

joy, elements underlying, 11
joyful learning
    choice/autonomy, role in, 14
    defined, 10–11
    noncognitive classes and, 10
    outcomes for learners
        impacting, 25–30

joyful learning *(cont'd)*
    reaching all students using,
        5–6
    understanding, 7–10
joyful learning framework (JLF).
    *See also* specific elements
    areas promoting, 11
    assessment and evaluation
        components, 11, 37
    implementing, reasons for,
        21–23
    learning environments and
        configurations in the, 48
    motivational generalizations
        in the, 11, 12–13*f*, 48
    overview, 14*f*

learner assessments
    by affective dimension,
        27–29*f*, 41*f*
    for belief in success, 27*f*, 31,
        32–33, 41
    Beyond Learners Survey for,
        37, 39*f*
    for desire for success,
        27–28*f*, 31, 32–33, 41*f*
    for expectations of success,
        27–28*f*, 27*f*
    Learner Profile and
        Instructional Responses,
        37, 38*f*
    Learner's Affective Dimen-
        sion Profile for, 37, 41*f*
    understanding requirements
        for success, 31, 32–33, 41*f*
learners
    contexts influencing, 22–23
    reaching all, 5–6
    successful, requirements
        for, 22
    the whole child focus, 22
Learner's Affective Dimension
    Profile, 41*f*
learning environments and
    configurations, supportive
    activities for, 48*f*. *See also*
    specific environments

lifelong learning, importance
    of, 8
locus of control, assessing, 29*f*,
    41*f*
low effort high-liked activities,
    19

Make a Difference Day, 50–51
meaning seekers, 18, 19
motivation
    assessing, 29*f*
    contexts influencing, 23
    engagement and, 17–21
    focus on, importance of,
        8–10
    instructional implications,
        12–13*f*
    in the JLF framework, 11,
        15–17
    noncognitive skills, effect
        on, 10
    outcomes for learners
        impacting, 25–30
    principles supporting, 16
    requirements for, 15
    responsibility for, 30
    valuing and, 13*f*
    variables, 21
motivational generalizations, 11,
    12–13*f*, 48. *See also* specific
    generalizations

No Child Left Behind Act, 9
noncognitive academic skills,
    2–3
noncognitive learning/classes
    achievement, effect on,
        9–10
    motivation, effect on, 10

Partnership for Assessment of
    Readiness for College and
    Careers (PARCC), 69
persistent learners, 18
physical environment
    activity: Artifact Displays,
        52

physical environment *(cont'd)*
    engagement and a safe,
        17, 68
    function of, 51
    in the JLF framework, 5, 11
    the structure: identity
        builders, 51–52
    supportive activities for, 48f
pleasure, types that prompt
    learning, 14
principled practice, 4

recognition, assessing, 28f, 41f
Response to Intervention (RTI)
    frameworks, 63–65, 64f
rigor, 66–67

school community
    activity: Make a Difference
        Day, 50–51
    goal of, 49–50
    in the JLF framework, 11
    joyful learning and the, 5
    purpose of focus on, 49
    the structure: schoolwide
        projects, 50–51
    supportive activities for, 48f
schoolwide factors, assessing
    and evaluating. *See also*
    teacher assessments
    Beyond Learners Survey for,
        43, 44–45f, 46f
    faculty and staff, 46f
    schoolwide vision, creating
        a, 35–36
    student success as basis
        for, 36
schoolwide projects, 50–51
self-efficacy
    assessing, 27f
    for engagement, 17

self-efficacy *(cont'd)*
    instructional implication, 12f
    in the JLF framework, 11
    pleasure and, 14
self-evaluation, benefits of, 65
Six Boxes, 53–55, 54f
small-group instruction
    activity: Connected Text
        Sets, 57–58
    function of, 56
    in the joyful learning
        framework, 11, 66
    the structure: group projects,
        56–58
    supportive activities for, 48f
Smarter Balanced Assessment
    Consortium, 69
social elements, assessing, 29f,
    41f
social relationships
    fun for building, 20
    pleasure and, 14
sociocultural context for
    motivation, 23
standardized tests, 9
standards, JLF correlation to,
    66–67
students. *See* learners
success
    in joyful learning, 5
    learning challenges and
        expectations of, 26
    noncognitive academic skills
        effect on, 9–10
success assessments
    affective outcomes, 34
    schoolwide factors, 36
    for students, 26, 27–29f
    for teachers, 31
    texts and materials, 32–33

teacher assessments
    Beyond Learners Survey, 43,
        44–45f
    intentionality, 30–31
    student success as basis
        for, 31
texts and materials, assessing
    selecting for affect on
        students, 31–32
    for student interaction with,
        32
    student success as basis for,
        32–33
text sets, 57

utility form of value, 13f

valuing
    defined, 13f
    for engagement, 17, 68
    importance, assessing, 28f,
        41f
    instructional implication, 13f
    motivation and, 13f

the whole child focus, 22
Whole Child Initiative, 22
whole-group instruction
    activity: Six Boxes, 53–55,
        54f
    engagement and, 52–53
    function of, 52
    in the JLF framework, 11, 66
    the structure: active
        participation and thinking,
        53–55, 54f
    supportive activities for, 48f

# About the Authors

**Michael F. Opitz** is professor emeritus of reading education at the University of Northern Colorado, where he taught undergraduate and graduate courses. An author and literacy consultant, Michael provides inservice and staff development sessions and presents at state and international conferences and also works with elementary school teachers to plan, teach, and evaluate lessons focused on different aspects of literacy. He is the author and coauthor of numerous books, articles, and reading programs.

**Michael P. Ford** is chair of and professor in the Department of Literacy and Language at the University of Wisconsin Oshkosh, where he teaches undergraduate and graduate courses. He is a former Title I reading and 1st grade teacher. Michael is the author of 5 books and more than 30 articles. Michael has worked with teachers throughout the country and his work with the international school network has included staff development presentations in the Middle East, Europe, Africa, South America, and Central America.

Friends and colleagues for more than two decades, Opitz and Ford began working together as a result of their common reading education interests. Through their publications and presentations, they continue to help educators reach readers through thoughtful, purposeful instruction grounded in practical theory.

# Related ASCD Resources:
## Engaging and Joyful Teaching and Learning

At the time of publication, the following ASCD resources were available (ASCD stock numbers appear in parentheses). For up-to-date information about ASCD resources, go to www.ascd.org.

### ASCD EDge Group

Exchange ideas and connect with other educators interested in differentiated instruction on the social networking site ASCD EDge™ at http://ascdedge.ascd.org.

### Print Products

*Building Learning Communities with Character: How to Integrate Academic, Social, and Emotional Learning*  Bernard Novick, Jeffrey S. Kress, and Maurice J. Elias (#101240)

*Curriculum 21: Essential Education for a Changing World*  edited by Heidi Hayes Jacobs (#109008)

*Create Success!: Unlocking the Potential of Urban Students*  Kadhir Rajagopal (#111022)

*Creating the Opportunity to Learn: Moving from Research to Practice to Close the Achievement Gap*  A. Wade Boykin and Pedro Noguera (#197157)

*Developing Habits of Mind in Elementary Schools: An ASCD Action Tool*  Karen Boyes and Graham Watts (#108015)

*Developing Habits of Mind in Secondary Schools: An ASCD Action Tool*  Karen Boyes and Graham Watts (#109108)

*Engaging the Whole Child: Reflections on Best Practices in Learning, Teaching, and Leadership*  edited by Marge Scherer and the Educational Leadership Staff (#109103)

*Everyday Engagement: Making Students and Parents Your Partners in Learning*  Katy Ridnouer (#109009)

*Flip Your Classroom: Reach Every Student in Every Class Every Day*  Jonathan Bergmann and Aaron Sams (#112060)

*The Formative Assessment Action Plan: Practical Steps to More Successful Teaching and Learning*  Nancy Frey and Douglas Fisher (#111013)

*Habits of Mind Across the Curriculum: Practical and Creative Strategies for Teachers*  edited by Arthur L. Costa and Bena Kallick (#108014)

*How to Create a Culture of Achievement in Your School and Classroom*  Douglas Fisher, Nancy Frey, and Ian Pumpian (#111014)

*Learning and Leading with Habits of Mind: 16 Essential Characteristics for Success*  edited by Arthur L. Costa and Bena Kallick (#108008)

*Promoting Social and Emotional Learning: Guidelines for Educators*  Maurice J. Elias, Joseph E. Zins, Roger P. Weissberg, Karin S. Frey, Mark T. Greenberg, Norris M. Haynes, Rachael Kessler, Mary E. Schwab-Stone, and Timothy P. Shriver (#197157)

 The Whole Child Initiative helps schools and communities create learning environments that allow students to be healthy, safe, engaged, supported, and challenged. To learn more about other books and resources that relate to the whole child, visit www.wholechildeducation.org.

For more information: send e-mail to member@ascd.org; call 1-800-933-2723 or 703-578-9600, press 2; send a fax to 703-575-5400; or write to Information Services, ASCD, 1703 N. Beauregard St., Alexandria, VA 22311-1714 USA.